ONTARIO MOUNTAIN BIKE TRAIL GUIDE

ONTARIO MOUNTAIN BIKE TRAIL GUIDE

Ron Seca

A BOSTON MILLS PRESS BOOK

Canadian Cataloguing in Publication Data

Seca, Ronald J., 1964-
The Ontario mountain bike trail guide

ISBN 1-55046-116-8

1. All terrain cycling - Ontario - Guidebooks.
2. Trails - Ontario - Guidebooks. 3. Ontario -
Guidebooks. I. Title.

GV1046.C22067 1994 796.6'4'09713 C94-930815-3

First published in 1994 by
Stoddart Publishing Co. Ltd.
34 Lesmill Road
Toronto, Canada
M3B 2T6
(416) 445-3333

A BOSTON MILLS PRESS BOOK
The Boston Mills Press
132 Main Street
Erin, Ontario
N0B 1T0

Cover design by Gillian Stead
Cover photograph courtesy of Adventure Photo/Masterfile
Interior design and maps by Ron Seca
Printed in Canada

The publisher gratefully acknowledges the support of the Canada Council, Ontario Ministry of Culture and Communications, Ontario Arts Council and Ontario Publishing Centre in the development of writing and publishing in Canada.

For Karen

may all your dreams come true

and for my family

Contents

Preface

The purpose of this book is to provide mountain bikers in Ontario with a way of finding trails to ride on. The experience of the author has been that these trails are very difficult to find unless someone tells you exactly where they are. Unless you have a lot of friends who mountain bike, chances are you have been riding on the same few trails all the time. This is the first and only book I know of that lists mountain-biking trails in Ontario.

This book has been three years in the making. I have spent thousands of hours and dollars collecting information, riding trails (tough life!), writing trail descriptions and designing trail maps.

I selected what I thought were forty-five of the best locations for mountain biking in Ontario. It was impossible to include all the trails that exist in Ontario. This guide details 117 trails, totalling over 1,000 kilometres. If you think I have missed an important trail, please write me a letter, care of the publisher, to tell me where it is, and I will try to include it in the next edition. My goal is to update this trail guide every two to three years.

Please respect the other trail users you encounter. This will ensure that others can enjoy the same trails as you. Always wear a helmet when you're biking, and bring a first-aid kit. You should also respect the environment. Think twice about crossing the next stream you encounter.

The information presented in this book was accurate at the time of printing. Check with local or regional authorities to make sure that mountain biking is still allowed in each area. The trails presented in this book are shared by outdoor enthusiasts for many other uses, such as hiking and horseback riding. Mountain biking is relatively new compared to these activities, and the managers of some land areas may change their minds and disallow mountain biking at any time if mountain biking conflicts with more well-established trail uses. The author and the publisher cannot be held responsible for any inconvenience you may suffer if you show up at one of these sites and find it has been closed to mountain bikers. As well, most of the trails located in conservation areas or provincial parks require an admission fee. Please check before you make plans!

I would like to thank all the Conservation Authorities, Ministry of Natural Resources offices, and municipal governments and their staff for their help in the completion of this book.

Reading the Trail Guide

The format of this book was carefully planned. Each trail map and description has a heading that tells you the name of the trail and/or the region it is located in. The trail name is followed by the name of the nearest major town or city, to help you to find the trail location easily on a map of Ontario. The number of trails and the total distance in kilometres for each trip are also provided. The directions you need to find the trail area are given next. Each trail is rated from easy to difficult. A rating of Easy/Difficult means that the location has both easy and difficult trails.

A description is included for each major trail. Distances are one-way unless noted by a ↔ symbol, which means the distance for the trail is round-trip. A round-trip distance means you will retrace your route to return to your starting point. Camping information is included for those of you who wish to stay at these excellent mountain-biking locations. I have also included telephone numbers for nearby hotels and resorts. This information will be valuable if you decide to visit these trail locations. Finally, I have included a contact number, so you can call each location to get additional information.

I wanted to keep the trail descriptions as brief as possible. In that way, this book differs from other bicycle route guidebooks, because they are usually very detailed and very boring. They tell you how to do everything and when to do it. These books are great for touring bicyclists but not for mountain bikers. My opinion is that mountain bikers are a unique breed who wish only to be pointed in the right direction and shown where to ride. They do not want to be told how to ride! For this reason I will leave the exploring of the individual trails to you, and I won't bore you with too many details. I have included all the essential details that most mountain bikers will need to find these trails. Have fun!

Ontario Mountain Bike Trail Guide
Trail Areas

Central Region Trails

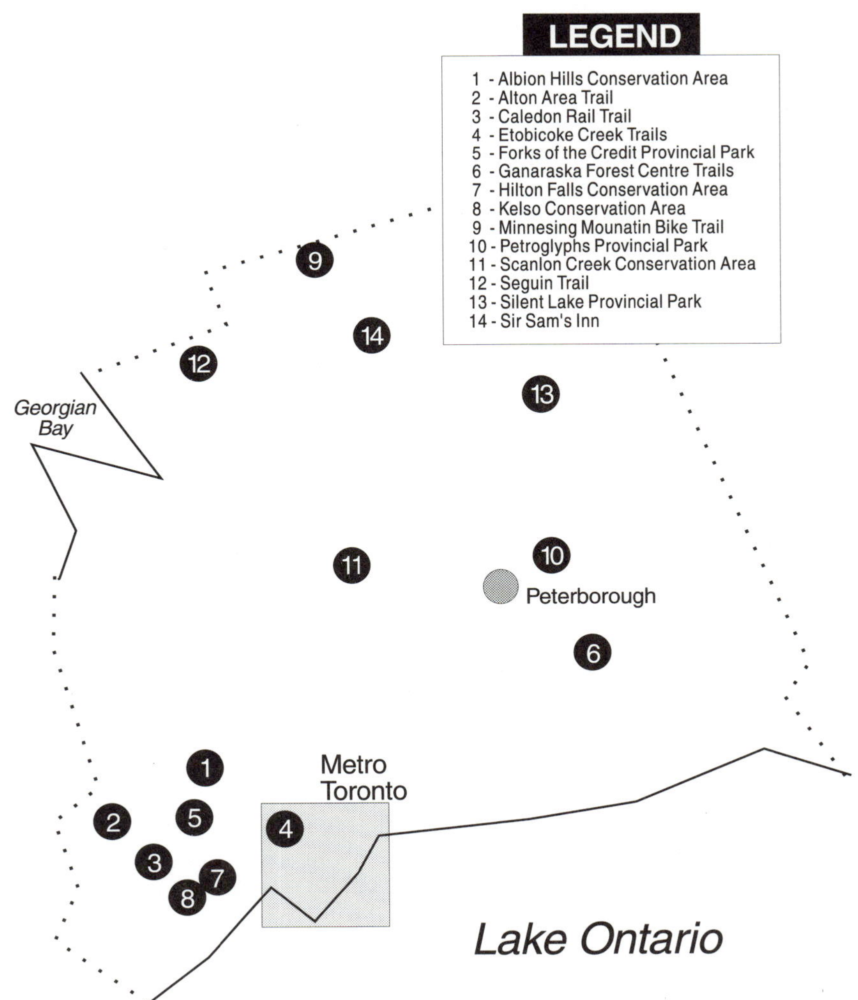

Albion Hills Conservation Area, Bolton

5 trails: 26.5 km

Location:

8 kilometres north of Bolton, 24 kilometres northwest of Toronto, off Highway 50. Park in the lot provided.

Rating: Easy/Difficult

The Trails

The beautiful 446-hectare Albion Hills Conservation Area is managed by the Metro Toronto and Region Conservation Authority (MTRCA). The MTRCA made a decision in the summer of 1993 to officially allow mountain-bike riding. I would advise you to phone the conservation authority at the number given here; they may be able to provide you with a new map. What are you waiting for?

If you are riding in the late spring or early summer, make sure you take along some insect repellent. The bugs can get quite thick in this conservation area. Be careful if you are using the trails on the weekends. There will be lots of other trail users at this time. Treat these trail users with respect and don't ruin it for others by giving the MTRCA any reasons to close these excellent trails down.

Albion Hills Conservation Area is a full-service recreational facility. Camping, picnicking, swimming and fishing facilities are superb. There are over 130 campsites.

The trail lengths are as follows:

Black Trail:	7 km
Blue Trail:	6 km
Green Trail:	2 km
Red Trail:	9 km
Yellow Trail:	2.5 km

I suggest you start your ride at the ski chalet. If you see a white blur fly past you on the Black Trail Loop, don't worry, it will just be me riding my faithful GT Avalanche.

Camping

Albion Hills Conservation Area (416) 661-6000
Indian Line Tourist Campground (905) 678-1233

Hotels/Resorts

Bolton Inn (905) 857-3382
Journey's End Motel (905) 452-0600
The Millcroft Inn (519) 941-8111

For more information contact:

Andrew Wickens, Manager
Metro Toronto and Region Conservation Authority
5 Shoreham Drive
Downsview, Ontario
M3N 1S4
(416) 661-6600

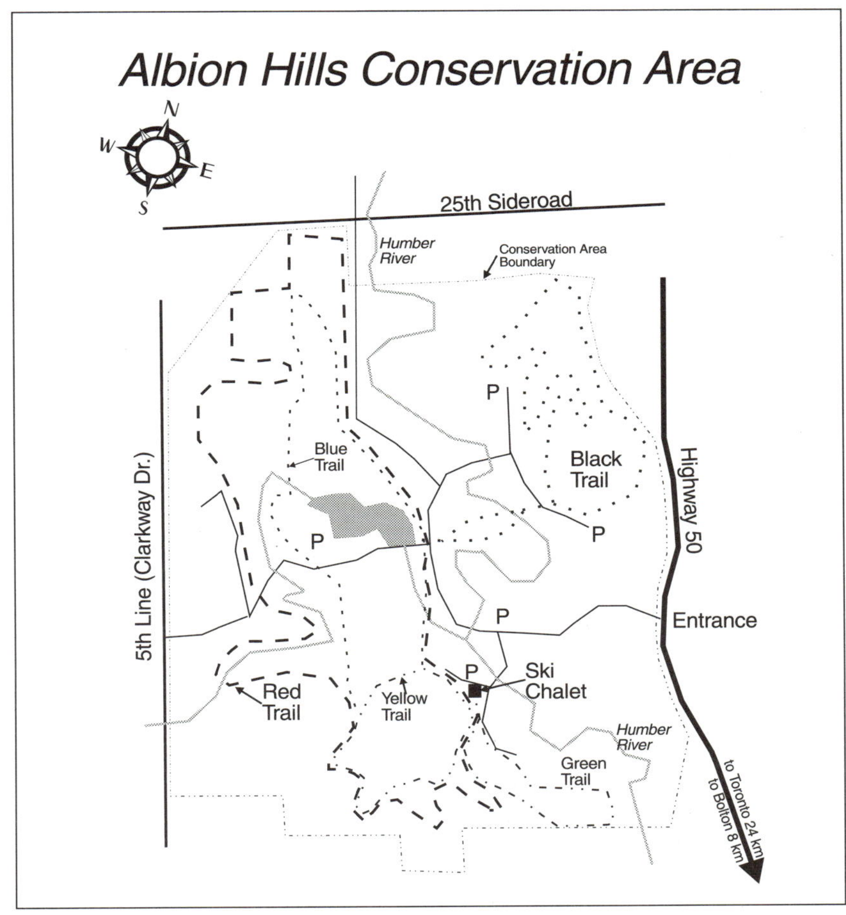

Alton Area Trail, Alton

1 trail: 10 km ↔

Location:

Located off Highway 136 in the town of Alton. Take Highway 24 west from Highway 10. Follow Highway 24 west until you reach Highway 136. Then follow Highway 136 north for 1.5 kilometres until you reach the entrance to an abandoned gravel pit on the right-hand side of the road.

Rating: Easy/Moderate

Main Trail

Park in the driveway of the gravel pit and start down the gravel road. Follow the trail through the gravel pit and across the train tracks. When you come to a parking lot with several old buildings, keep to the left and follow the gravel road north. The road parallels the railroad tracks for 2 kilometres. You will have to cross a road to continue on the trail. Once across the road, the trail follows a fire access road for about 1.5 kilometres into the town of Alton.

If you feel like a challenge, you can go into Alton and, at the point where Highway 136 turns east, follow a road north. This road climbs the Niagara Escarpment and you should get an excellent view of the surrounding countryside when you reach the top.

Camping

Monora Conservation Area (905) 451-1615
Summer Place Park (519) 928-5408
Terra Cotta Conservation Area (905) 877-9650

Hotels/Resorts

Cataract Inn (519) 927-3033
Orangeville Motel (519) 941-6831
The Millcroft Inn (519) 941-8111

Alton Area Trail
Town of Alton
End
P
N
W
E
S
Highway 136
Ponds
Credit River
Highway 10
P
Start
Highway 24
Town of Caledon

Caledon Rail Trail, Caledon

1 trail: 70 km ↔

Location:

This trail starts in Terra Cotta and follows an abandoned railway bed to its end at Highway 9 in Palgrave. Parking is available at the Terra Cotta conservation area and in communities along the trail.

Rating: Moderate

The Trail

The Caledon Rail Trail runs alongside the defunct Hamilton & Northwestern Railway, built in the 1870s. In 1989 the town of Caledon acquired the land and designated it for passive recreational uses such as walking, hiking, mountain biking and horseback riding. Mountain bikers and horseback riders should give way to pedestrians on this sometimes busy trail.

The trail starts in the village of Terra Cotta. You will travel over the Niagara Escarpment, the Credit River, the Oak Ridges Moraine and the Humber River. The terrain is composed of gravel terraces and glacial spillways. Vegetation is typical of the Great Lakes hardwoods region. If you are lucky, you might see some of the wildlife that lives along this trail, such as deer, coyotes, beaver, fox, hawks and snapping turtles.

Be careful when you cross concession roads and be extremely careful when crossing Highway 10, Highway 50 and the 20th Sideroad. These roads are very busy and should be crossed with extreme caution.

The trail ends at Highway 9. If you are feeling adventurous, turn around and ride back to Terra Cotta. I hope you enjoy this excellent trail. If you would like to volunteer to help work on the trail, or to donate money for trail maintenance, contact the Caledon Parks and Recreation Department at the number on page 11.

Camping

Albion Hills Conservation Area (905) 661-6000
Monora Conservation Area (905) 451-1615
Terra Cotta Conservation Area (905) 877-9650

Hotels/Resorts

Cataract Inn (519) 927-3033
Orangeville Motel (519) 941-6831
The Millcroft Inn (519) 941-8111

For more information contact:

Graham Burke, Director of Parks and Recreation
Town of Caledon
P.O. Box 1000
200 Church Street
Caledon East, Ontario
L0N 1E0
(905) 584-2273

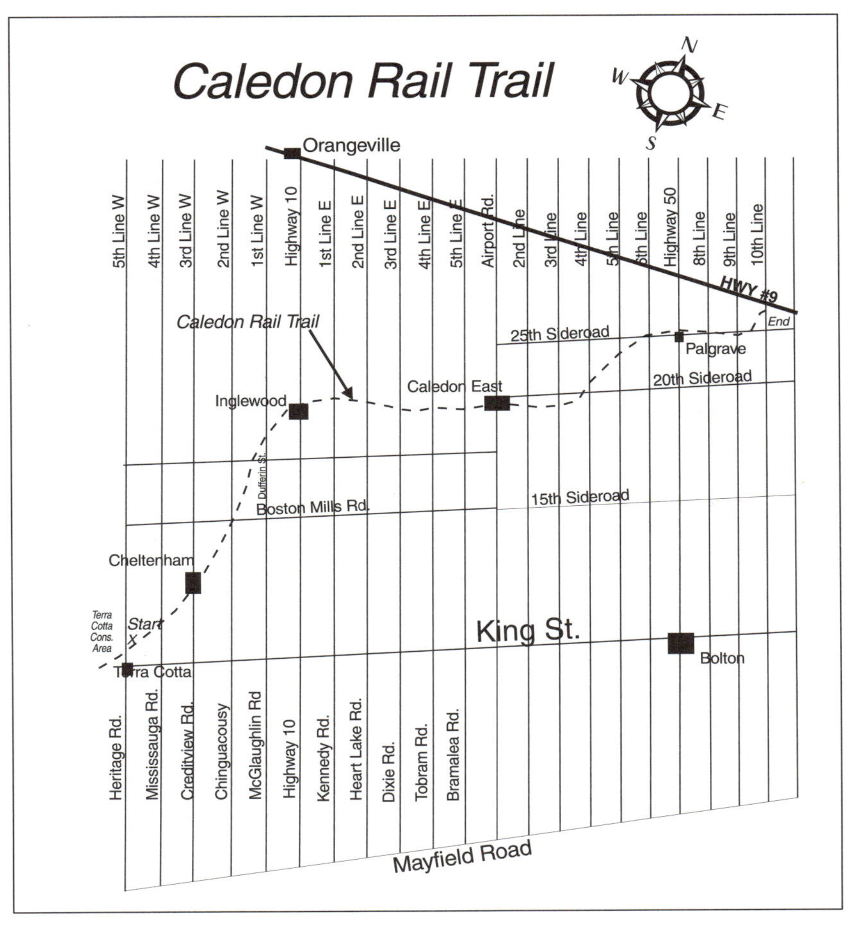

Etobicoke Creek Trails, Etobicoke

3 trails: 19 km ↔

Location:

Renforth Drive and Rathburn Road, Etobicoke.

Rating: Moderate

Main Trail: 9 km

Park at the Etobicoke Olympium on Rathburn Road just west of Renforth Drive. Turn right onto Rathburn Road as you leave the Olympium parking lot and head west for about 1 kilometre to a three-way intersection. Cross the road to where the dead-end sign and barrier are located. The trail starts about 30 metres from this point in the forest. The first 400 metres of the trail is a single track that follows the edge of the Etobicoke Creek valley. As you leave the forest, keep to the left and ride through the City of Etobicoke leaf-composting site.

The trail continues down a steep valley access road. Turn right at the bottom of the road and follow the trail until you come to the Eglinton Avenue bridge. You have now ridden 2 kilometres. Continue following the trail under the bridge until you reach a stream crossing Etobicoke Creek. The creek is usually about knee-deep and is easy to cross. Once you reach the other side of the creek, follow the trail through a difficult rutted area until you come to a second creek. This crossing is a little harder and you may want to dismount and walk your bike across.

Continue to follow the trail once you reach the other side of the creek and soon you will reach the Highway 401 bridge. Continue under the bridge, and the trail soon ends at the boundary of Pearson International Airport. Turn around and backtrack the way you came, prepared to ride some of the better side trails you may have seen on the way.

Side Trail One: 7 km

You will find a trail that travels up the side of the valley just south the Highway 401 bridge. You can follow this trail at the top of the Etobicoke Creek valley until you reach Eglinton Avenue. Cross the road and continue on the trail until you reach the place where you started, at the bottom of a steep access road. The last 30 metres of this trail are hard to follow, so be careful.

Side Trail Two: 3 km

At a point halfway between the first and second stream crossing, look for a trail going up the west side of the valley. Follow the trail up the side of the valley (if you can!) and ride this trail until its end.

There are numerous other side trails that I haven't described. I will leave the exploration of these trails to you. These trails are great for practising your technical skills.

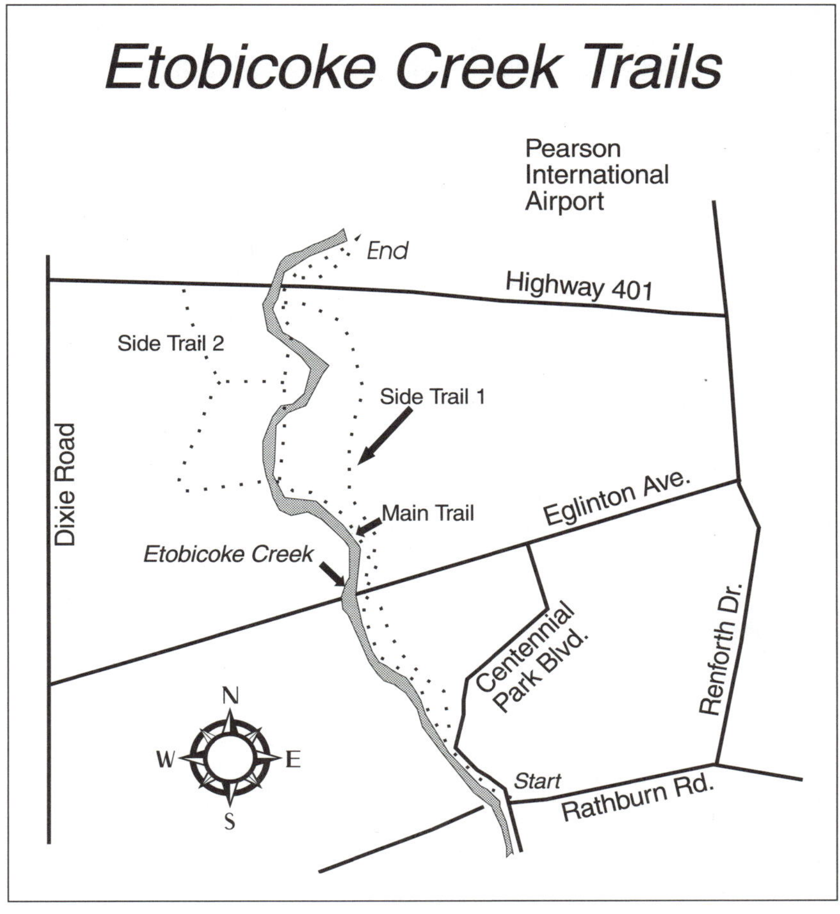

f the Credit Provincial Park, Belfountain

.5 km ↔

Location:

The Forks of the Credit Road at the Forks of the Credit River. Take the Forks of the Credit Road west from Highway 10. Follow this road until you reach a green bridge at the Forks of the Credit River. Cross the bridge and follow the gravel road a short way until you reach one of the two Ministry of Natural Resources parking lots on the left side of the road.

Rating: Easy

Main Trail: 4.5 km

Park in the parking lots and unpack your bike. Follow the gravel road north for 500 metres until you reach the Forks of the Credit Provincial Park. The main trail starts off as a fire access road and you will follow it for approximately 1,500 metres. When the road ends, follow a trail up the side of the valley wall. You will have to carry your bike down a set of stairs. Follow the trail until you come to the Cataract. The Credit River flows over the Niagara Escarpment at this point, forming the Cataract. This is the site of an old hydro-electric station. The natural waterfall was dammed up in the early 1900s, but the power station is no longer being used. Take a few moments to view the spectacular scenery and then head back the way you came.

Secondary Trail: 750 metres

This trail starts halfway down the access road. Follow this trail through the forest and watch out for poison ivy! You will come out in a meadow and you can follow the trail along the side of the Credit River. This is a nice place to have a snack. Watch for beaver on this trail. Follow the trail until you join with the main trail at the point where the fire access road ends.

Camping

No camping is allowed in this park unless you are hiking on the Bruce Trail, which goes through this area.

Monora Conservation Area (905) 451-1615
Summer Place Park (519) 928-5408
Terra Cotta Conservation Area (905) 877-9650

Hotels/Resorts

Cataract Inn (519) 927-3033
Orangeville Motel (519) 941-6831
The Millcroft Inn (519) 941-8111

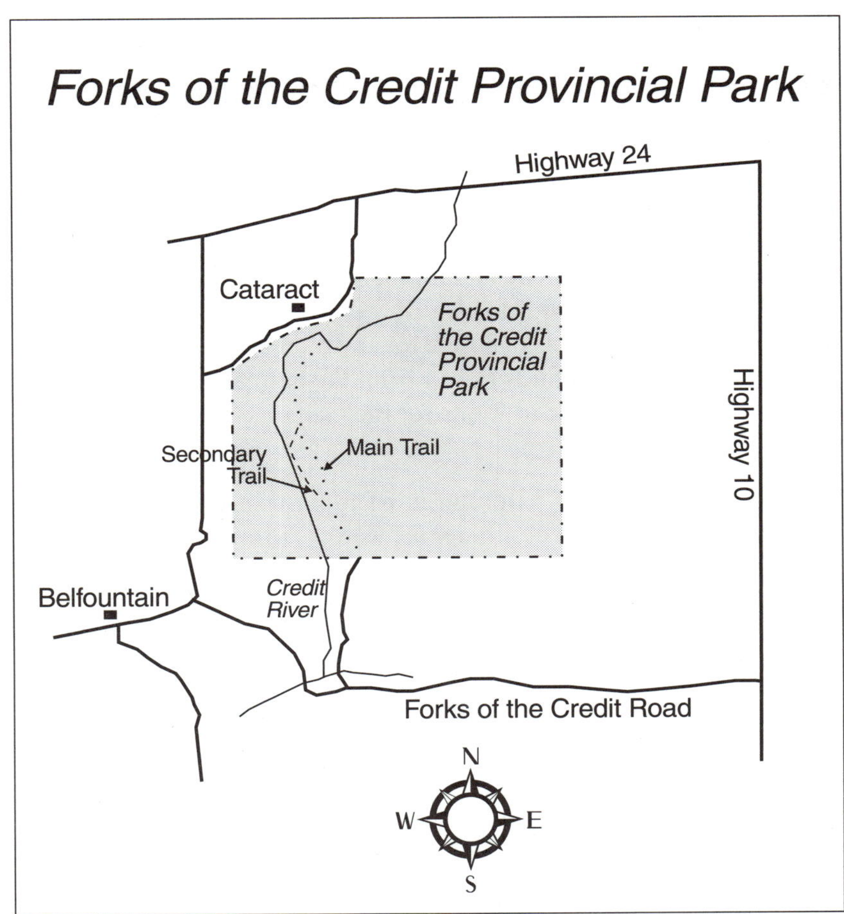

6 trails: 30 km

Location:

Southwest of Peterborough. Follow Highway 35/115 and exit at County Road 9. Follow this road east for 6 kilometres through the town of Kendall. Continue east on this road for another 3 kilometres and turn left (north) onto a sideroad at the Newscastle–Hope Township boundary. Follow this sideroad north for about 4 kilometres until you reach the Ganaraska Forest Centre and park your car there.

Rating: Moderate/Difficult

The Trails

The Ganaraska Forest is 4,400 hectares in size and consists of a mixture of natural hardwood and plantation forest. Numerous forest access roads can be ridden in addition to the six trails in the Forest Centre.

I strongly suggest that you contact the Ganaraska Region Conservation Authority for a membership and a comprehensive colour map of the Ganaraska Forest that includes all its forest roads and trails. The colour map can be picked up at the Forest Centre or sent to you if you purchase an annual membership. The annual memberships fees are $15.00 for an individual and $25.00 for a family. Your membership provides unlimited use of the Ganaraska Forest for any recreational activity except cross-country skiing. Funds raised from the annual membership program provide badly needed funds for the Ganaraska Forest and maintenance of the trail system.

There are hundreds of kilometres of mountain-bike trails in the Ganaraska Forest. You could spend weeks riding them.

Because the forest is quite remote, I suggest you ride this area with a partner, and bring a first-aid kit, food, and lots of water. You should also wear long pants, as the poison ivy is quite thick at times.

Park at the Forest Centre (see map) and start having some fun. These trails should challenge even the most experienced mountain bikers. Be sure to pick up the detailed trail map for the six trails at the Forest Centre. Membership applications are available from the Ganaraska Region Conservation Authority at the number given on the next page.

Camping

Beavermead Park (705) 742-9712
Hope Mill Conservation Area (705) 745-5791

Hotels/Resorts

Journey's End Motel (705) 748-6801
Otonabee Inn (705) 742-3454

For more information contact:

Ganaraska Region Conservation Authority
P.O. Box 328
Port Hope, Ontario L1A 3W4
(905) 885-8173

16 km of trails

Location:

The Hilton Falls Conservation Area is located at 4985 Campbellville Sideroad, Milton. Exit Highway 401 at Guelph Line. Follow Guelph Line north for a short way and turn right at the Campbellville Sideroad. Follow this road for a few kilometres until you reach the entrance to the conservation area.

Rating: Easy/Moderate

The Trails

In May 1992 the Halton Region Conservation Authority approved the designation of specific trails for mountain biking in Hilton Falls Conservation Area for a one-year trial period. The authority will probably be reexamining the mountain-bike issue from time to time. As of early February 1994, mountain biking is still allowed access. I would advise you to phone the conservation authority to avoid any disappointment.

Mountain bikers must use the main entrance and pay the entrance fee to use the conservation area. A permit will be issued and this must be displayed on your mountain bike at all times. You must stay on the trails that have been marked for use by mountain bikers. If you ride on any of the other trails, your permit will be revoked and you may be fined. Continued access to these fine trails requires the co-operation of everyone riding these trails.

The trails or portions thereof may be closed during wet or soft conditions in spring, and at times when mountain-bike activity may be incompatible with other activities. Please respect all trail closings, especially those due to wet weather.

Camping

Guelph Lake Conservation Area (519) 824-5061
Milton Heights Campground (905) 878-6781
Terra Cotta Conservation Area (905) 877-9650

Hotels/Resorts

Fifth Wheel Truck Stops (905) 878-8441
Heritage Inn (905) 878-2855
Mohawk Inn (905) 854-2277

For more information contact:

Halton Region Conservation Authority
2596 Britannia Road West
R.R. 2
Milton, Ontario
L9T 2X6
(905) 336-1158

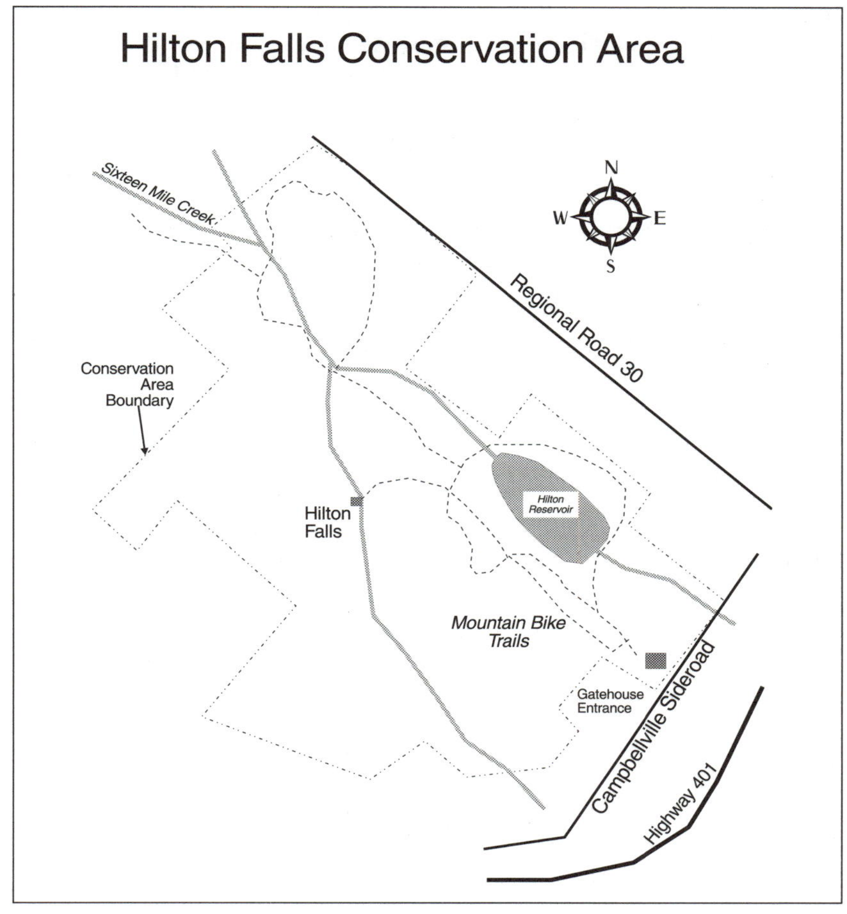

10 km of trails

Location:

The Kelso Conservation Area is located at number 5255, 3rd Sideroad in Milton. Exit Highway 401 at Highway 25. Follow Highway 25 south for a few kilometres until you reach Steeles Avenue. Turn right onto Steeles Avenue and follow it until you reach Regional Road 22. Turn right and follow this road for a few kilometres until you reach the entrance to the conservation area at Regional Road 28.

Rating: Moderate/Difficult

The Trails

In May 1992 the Halton Region Conservation Authority approved the designation of specific trails for mountain biking in Kelso Conservation Area for a one-year trial period. The authority will probably be reexamining the mountain-bike issue from time to time. As of early February 1994, mountain biking is still allowed access. I would advise you to phone the conservation authority to avoid any disappointment.

Mountain bikers must use the main entrance and pay the entrance fee to use the conservation area. A permit will be issued and this must be displayed on your mountain bike at all times. You must stay on the trails that have been marked for use by mountain bikers. If you ride on any of the other trails, your permit will be revoked and you may be fined. Continued access to these trails requires the co-operation of everyone riding them.

The trails or portions thereof may be closed during wet or soft conditions in spring and at times when mountain-bike activity may be incompatible with activities. Please respect all trail closings, especially those due to wet weather.

Camping

Guelph Lake Conservation Area (519) 824-5061
Milton Heights Campground (905) 878-6781
Terra Cotta Conservation Area (905) 877-9650

Hotels/Resorts

Fifth Wheel Truck Stops (905) 878-8441
Heritage Inn (905) 878-2855
Mohawk Inn (905) 854-2277

For more information contact:

Halton Region Conservation Authority
2596 Britannia Road West
R.R. 2
Milton, Ontario
L9T 2X6
(905) 336-1158

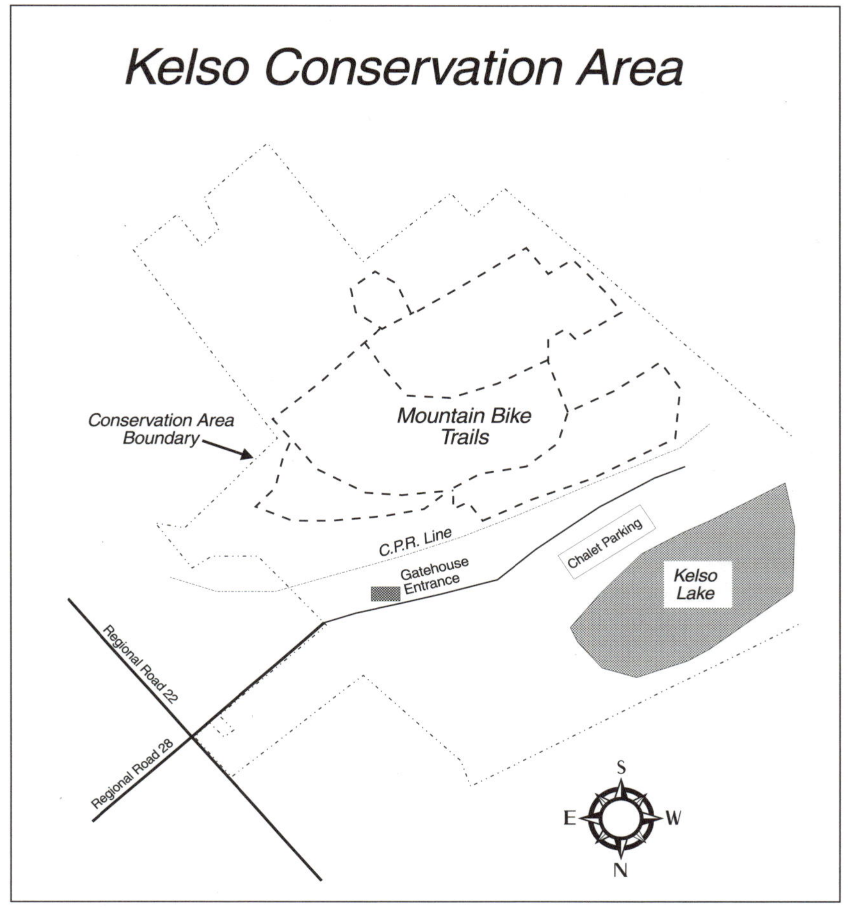

3 trail loops: 32 km

Location:

Algonquin Park, just off Highway 60 near Canisbay Lake. The trail is located 23 kilometres from the West Gate of the park.

Rating: Moderate

The Trail

The Minnesing Mountain Bike Trail is named after the Minnesing Road, which ran from the Highland Inn on Cache Lake to Minnesing Lodge on Burnt Island Lake. The only access to this luxury wilderness lodge was a 16-kilometre ride on the bumpy Minnesing Road. The lodge was eventually torn down in the 1950s.

All three trail loops start at the parking lot just off Highway 60. The trail lengths are 5 km, 10 km, and 17 km. Shelters are located at the start of trail loop 1 and on the return leg of trail loop 2. An emergency supply barrel is located at the halfway point of trail loop 3. The barrel contains a first-aid kit, food, a sleeping bag, blankets, and matches and kindling. Please let the Park staff know if you use up any of these emergency supplies. The nearest hospital is located in Hunstville (705-789-2311).

Make sure to adhere to the Algonquin Park regulations such as no overnight camping along the trails and no mountain-bike riding on the canoe portages. The trail is open from mid-June to Thanksgiving. For use at other times of the year contact the East Gate Information Office. This is one ride you will not want to miss!

Camping

Algonquin Provincial Park, Canisbay (705) 633-5572
Algonquin Provincial Park, Kearney Lake (705) 633-5572

Hotels/Resorts

Blue Water Acres (705) 635-2880
Grandview Inn (705) 789-4417
Sir Sam's Inn (705) 754-2188

For more information contact:

Algonquin Provincial Park
East Gate Information Office
(705) 633-5572

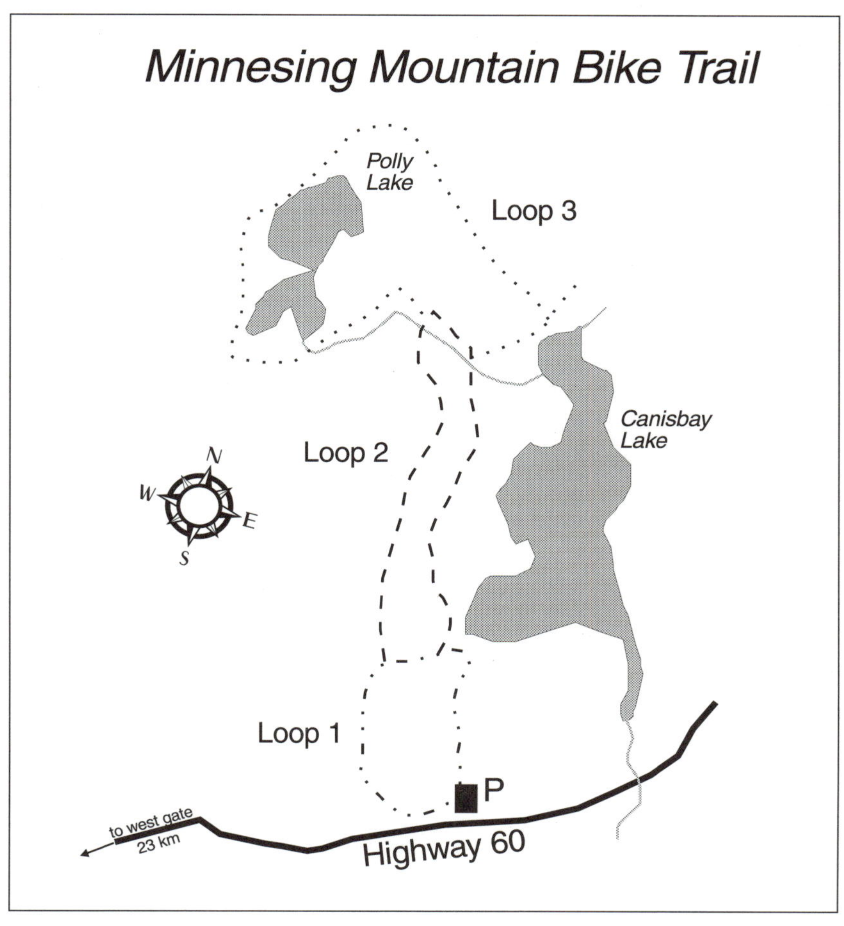

2 trails: 13 km

Location:

11 kilometres east on Northey's Bay Road from Highway 28, near Woodview. One-half hour northeast of Peterborough.

Rating: Easy/Difficult

Petroglyphs Provincial Park

This park contains one of the largest concentrations of native rock carvings in Canada. These petroglyphs are thought to have been carved by Algonquin-speaking natives five hundred to a thousand years ago. Be sure to stop and examine some of these extraordinary carvings.

The vegetation in the park is typical of Great Lakes–St. Lawrence lowlands forest regions. The park area is made up of large stands of red and white pine interspersed with pockets of spruce and mixed hardwoods such as white birch, sugar maple and red oak. Damming by beavers has created a number of active wetlands within the park. During the spring and summer a wide variety of colourful wildflowers covers the surrounding landscape. Make sure you pack your insect repellent if you visit the park during the spring or early summer.

High Falls Trail: 6.5 km ↔

This trail begins at the north end of the parking area. Follow the trail around the scenic Minnow Lake and on to High Falls on Eels Creek. This trail meanders through a variety of interesting areas, including rocky ridges, wetlands, and conifer and deciduous forests. Keep your eyes open for beaver and otter on your way.

Main Trail: 6.5 km

This trail starts at the same place as the High Falls Trail. Follow this trail around the marsh to the High Falls Trail. You may also take an alternate route and ride down to McGinnis Lake.

Camping

Algonquin Provincial Park, Canisbay (705) 633-5572
Silent Lake Provincial Park (613) 339-2807

Hotels/Resorts

Sir Sam's Inn (705) 754-2188
Stricker's Resort (705) 654-3547

For more information contact:

District Manager
Ministry of Natural Resources
P.O. Box 500
Bancroft, Ontario
K0L 1C0
(613) 332-3940
or Park Office (705) 877-2552

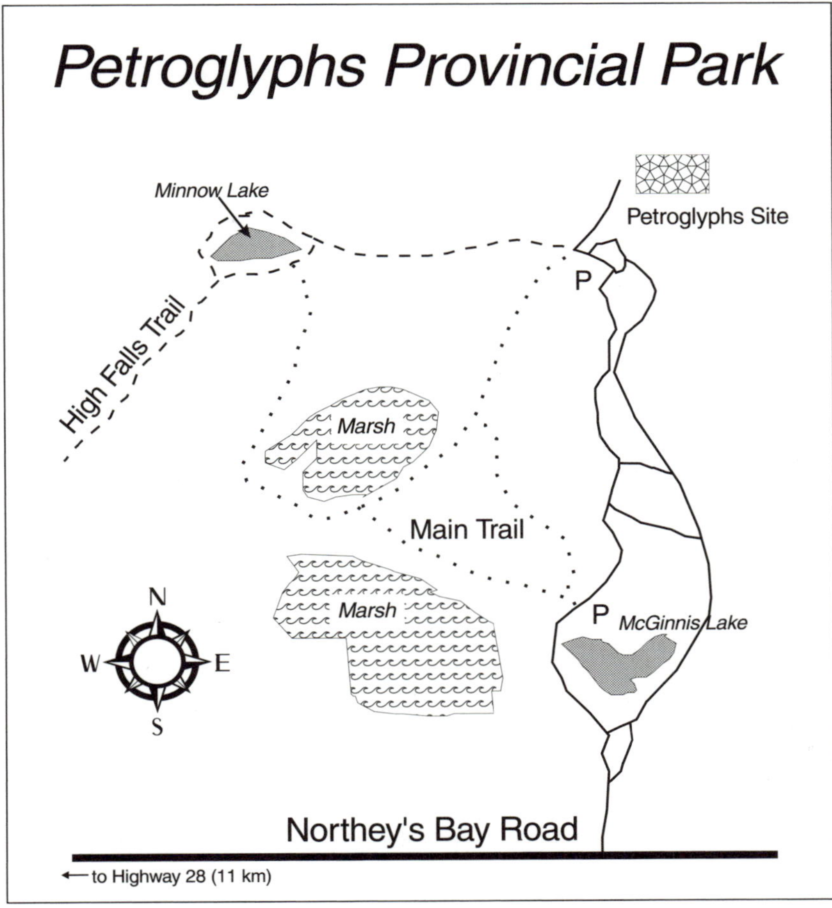

Scanlon Creek Conservation Area, Bradford

1 trail: 13 km

Location:

Scanlon Creek Conservation Area is located just off 9th Line. Exit Highway 11 at 9th Line and follow this road for about 500 metres until you come to the entrance to the conservation area. The conservation area is located about 4 kilometres north of Bradford.

Rating: Easy

Main Trail: 13 km

The trail starts at the education centre and follows Scanlon Creek up to the reservoir and past the dam at the east end of the conservation area. Follow the trail around the other side of the reservoir and along the other side of the creek back to the education centre. You may also want to ride on some of the side trails you encounter along your way.

The trail gives you excellent views of the 283 hectares of woodlands and meadows of the conservation area. Watch for tracks of white-tailed deer on the trails and keep a lookout for muskrat in the marshy areas.

Camping

Earl Rowe Provincial Park (705) 435-4331
Oro Camping (705) 487-2610
Sibbald Point Provincial Park (905) 722-8061

Hotels/Resorts

Bradford Motel (905) 775-6661
Comfort Motel (905) 775-2034
Journey's End Motel (705) 722-3600

For more information contact:

Manager
Lake Simcoe Region Conservation Authority
P.O. Box 282
Newmarket, Ontario
L3Y 4X1
(905) 895-1281
or Zenith: 38250 (toll-free)

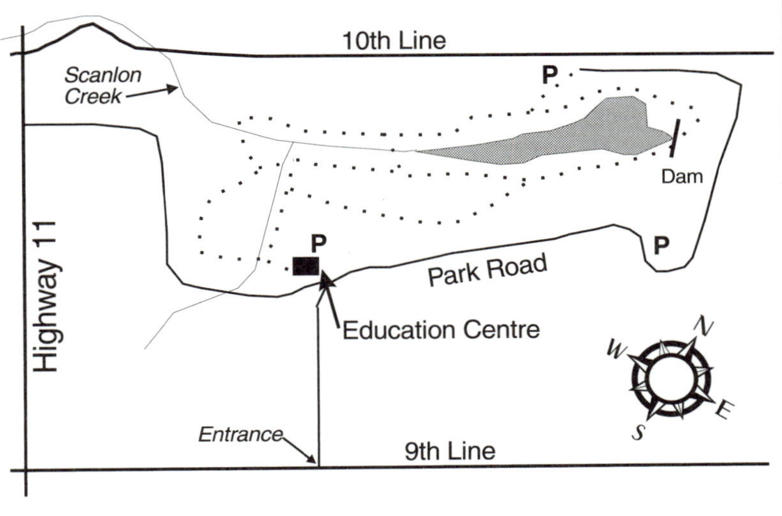

Seguin Trail, Parry Sound

1 trail: 122 km ↔

Location:

This trail is located about 12 kilometres south of Parry Sound. The easiest access is from the Ontario Tourism Office, which is located 6 kilometres south of Oastler Lake Provincial Park on the east side of Highway 69. Access is also available on the Fern Glen Road 6 kilometres west of Highway 11 and 8 kilometres north of Novar. The trail crosses Highway 518 at several points and all intersections have been posted.

Rating: Difficult

Seguin Trail

The trail travels the path of the old Arnprior & Parry Sound Railway and is a relatively easy but long ride. Due to its round-trip length of 122 kilometres, it should only be attempted by experienced mountain bikers. This trail is heavily used at times by ATVs and horseback riders. Make sure you give way to these and other users of the trail. Watch out for sandy areas of the trail. Make sure you bring lots of food and water and a first-aid kit, since this trail is fairly remote. Don't forget your insect repellent in the spring and early summer, or you will be the main course.

In the 1890s lumber magnate J.R. Booth constructed the railway to move lumber from the vast tracts of land lying between the upper reaches of the Ottawa River and Georgian Bay to the once-thriving shipping terminal of Depot Harbour on Parry Island. Before the line was discontinued in 1955, communities along the route, such as Swords and Seguin Falls, boomed while serving both the lumbering industry and American tourists seeking wilderness adventures.

When shipping lines moved south in the 1900s these towns and others settled down to become quiet backwaters, and Depot Harbour not only lost its shipping significance, it eventually burned and became the ghost town now visible on Parry Island.

The trail cuts laterally across the Canadian Shield and features exposed rock formations, indigenous forests, and glimpses of shy wildlife, from freeloading chipmunks to soaring hawks.

Camping

Arrowhead Provincial Park (705) 789-5105
Oastler Lake Provincial Park (705) 378-2401

Hotels/Resorts

Arrowhead Motor Inn (705) 789-7307
Journey's End Motel (705) 746-6221

For more information contact:

Ministry of Natural Resources
4 Miller Street
Parry Sound, Ontario P2A 1S8
(705) 746-4201

3 Trails: 19.5 km

Location:

Silent Lake Provincial Park is located approximately one-half hour by car south of Bancroft, off Highway 28.

Rating: Easy/Difficult

Lakeshore Hiking Trail: 15 km

This trail roughly follows the outline of Silent Lake. This is a great trail for mountain bikers in good shape. You will have to carry your bike over several sections. You may want to avoid this trail during wet periods, as it can get quite muddy. Bring lots of water and watch out for poison ivy!

The trail begins at the day-use area at the head of Silent Lake and takes you through beautiful beaver meadows, hardwood forests and cedar–black ash swamps. There are colourful rock-cuts on this trail. Keep your eyes open so you can yield the right of way to the occasional moose.

Remember to have fun and leave the trail as you found it, so others can enjoy this unique trail. Before you know it you will be back where you started. If you want some easier trails, try the next two out for size.

Lakehead Loop Trail: 1.5 km

This trail is accessible from either the day-use area or Granite Ridge Campgrounds. It starts at the bridge crossing Silent Creek, just to the east of the open area at the head of Silent Lake. Follow the trail along the lakeshore. The trail makes its way to higher ground through stands of hemlock, sugar maple, and red oak. The trail then descends through a rocky area and doubles back on itself to finish where you started off.

Bonnie's Trail: 3 km

The trail starts at the Pincer Bay parking lot. This trail winds past many unique and interesting features. You may also see a beaver or a mink if you ride quietly enough.

Camping

Silent Lake Provincial Park (613) 339-2807
The Homestead (613) 339-2500

Hotels/Resorts

Birch Cliff Lodge (613) 332-3316
Forest View Lodge (613) 332-3173
Sir Sam's Inn (705) 754-2188

For more information contact:

Ministry of Natural Resources
P.O. Box 500
Bancroft, Ontario K0L 1C0
(613) 332-3940

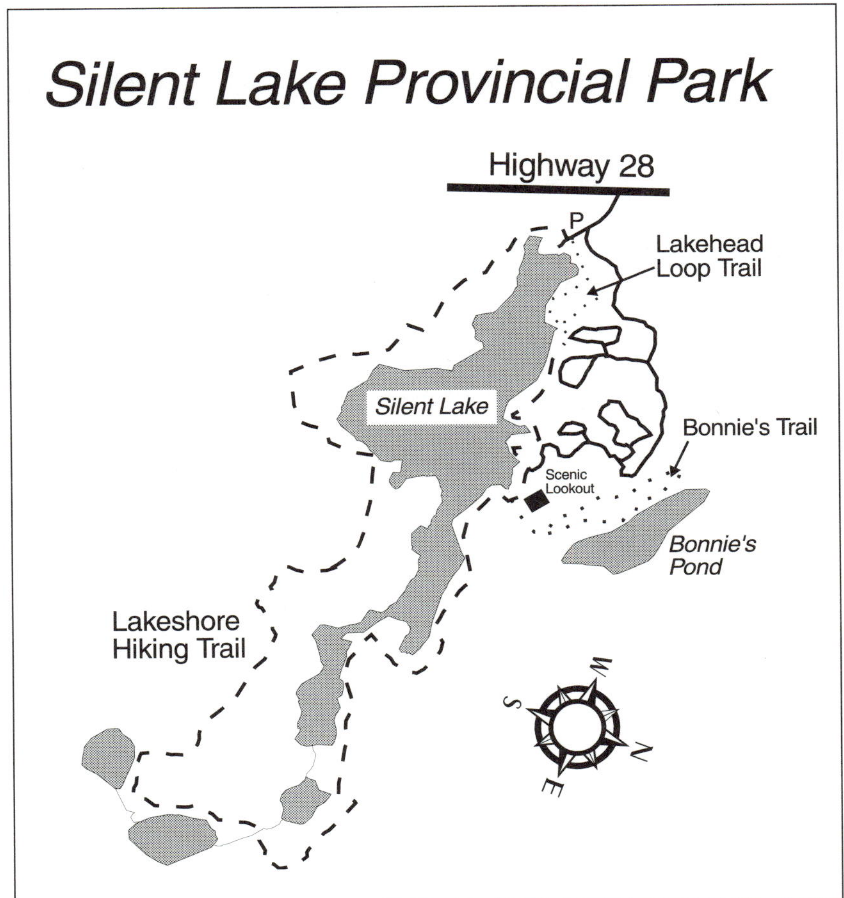

Sir Sam's Inn, Eagle Lake

4 trails: 26 km +

Location:

Eagle Lake in the Haliburton Highlands. Follow Highway 118 northwest of the village of Haliburton for 6 kilometres. Exit off Highway 118 onto County Road 6. Follow County Road 6 for 8 kilometres until you come to Sir Sam's Road. Follow this road up to the resort and enjoy.

Rating: Moderate/Difficult

The Trails

The starting point for all the trails is at the picturesque Sir Sam's Inn, a historic lakeside estate built circa 1917. Luxury accommodations and superb dining await you at the end of an invigorating ride. All the trails climb, twist and turn through glade forest up to the open plateau, at times providing breathtaking views over Eagle and Moose lakes. The trail changes from hard pack to gravel to grass. Deer, rabbits and partridge are common sights. Just some of the possibilities are shown on the map. Feel free to explore.

Basshaunt Lake Loop:	3 km
Beaver Pond Trail:	8.5 km
North Road Trip:	10 km
Village Visit:	4 km
Fitness Trail:	0.5 km

Camping

Edgewater Beach Resort (705) 457-2277
Haliburton Forest and Wild Life Reserve (705) 754-2198
Silver Beach Camping Park (705) 457-1429

Hotels/Resorts

Sir Sam's Inn (all-inclusive) (705) 754-2188
Silver Eagle Resort (housekeeping) (705) 754-2497

For more information contact:

Haliburton Highlands Chamber of Commerce
Box 147
Minden, Ontario
K0M 2K0
1-800-461-7677

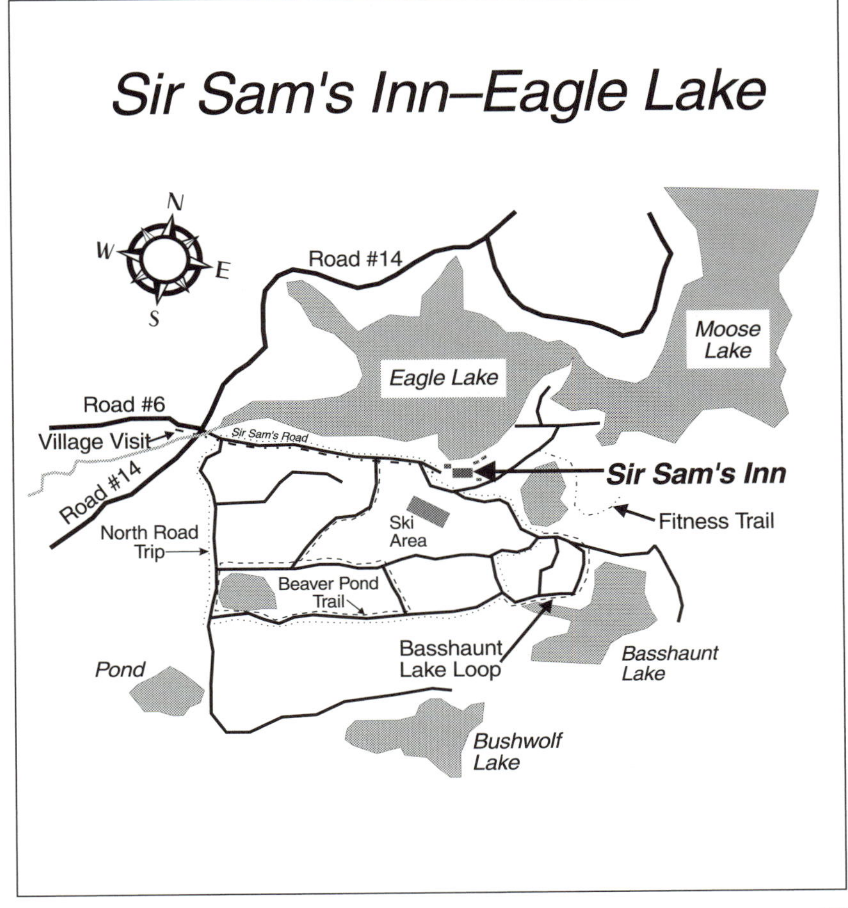

Northern Region Trails

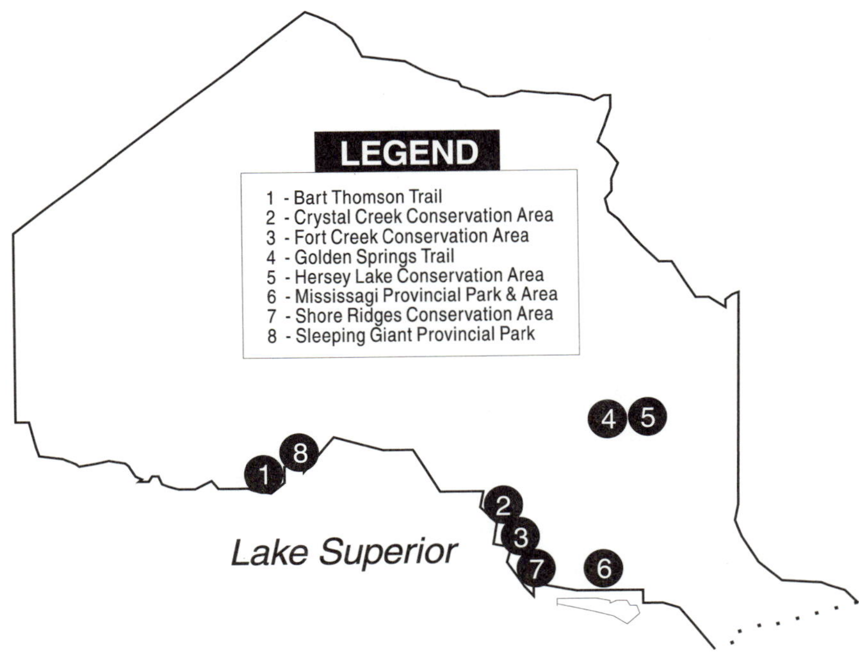

2 trails: 14.5 km

Location:

Off Highway 101 in Porcupine and South Porcupine. Access can be gained from the parking lot at the north end of Porcupine Lake.

Rating: Easy/Moderate

North Loop: 6 km

Starting at the parking lot at the north end of Porcupine Lake, the trail crosses Highway 101 and passes through a perimeter fence of the Resource Centre. The trail then follows the service road to the northern boundary of the centre, enters the bush, and emerges at the Broulan Reef Road. The trail continues westward, crossing two hydro lines, to Davidson Road, which it follows south for 500 metres. The trail then reenters the bush. From here it continues westward, emerging at the end of Legion Drive. Riding on Legion Drive and Golden Avenue, you can reach the west shore of Porcupine Lake and join up with the south loop of the trail.

South Loop: 8.5 km

Again starting at the north end of Porcupine Lake, the trail strikes east through Bannerman Park along Bourke Avenue, Haileybury Crescent and Lovers Lane to Back Road, and then along the south shore of the lake. The trail finally emerges at Evans Street and heads north, running along the lakeside and through the Northern College grounds.

It joins up with the north loop after following along Highway 101 and Bristol Road.

Camping

Horseshoe Lake (705) 268-2033
Kettle Lake Provincial Park (705) 267-7951

Hotels/Resorts

Carabelle Motel (705) 235-8101
Journey's End Motel (705) 264-9474
Trillium Motel and Cabins (705) 235-3839

For more information contact:

Mattagami Region Conservation Authority
Civic Centre
133 Cedar Street South
Timmins, Ontario
P4N 2G9
(705) 264-5309

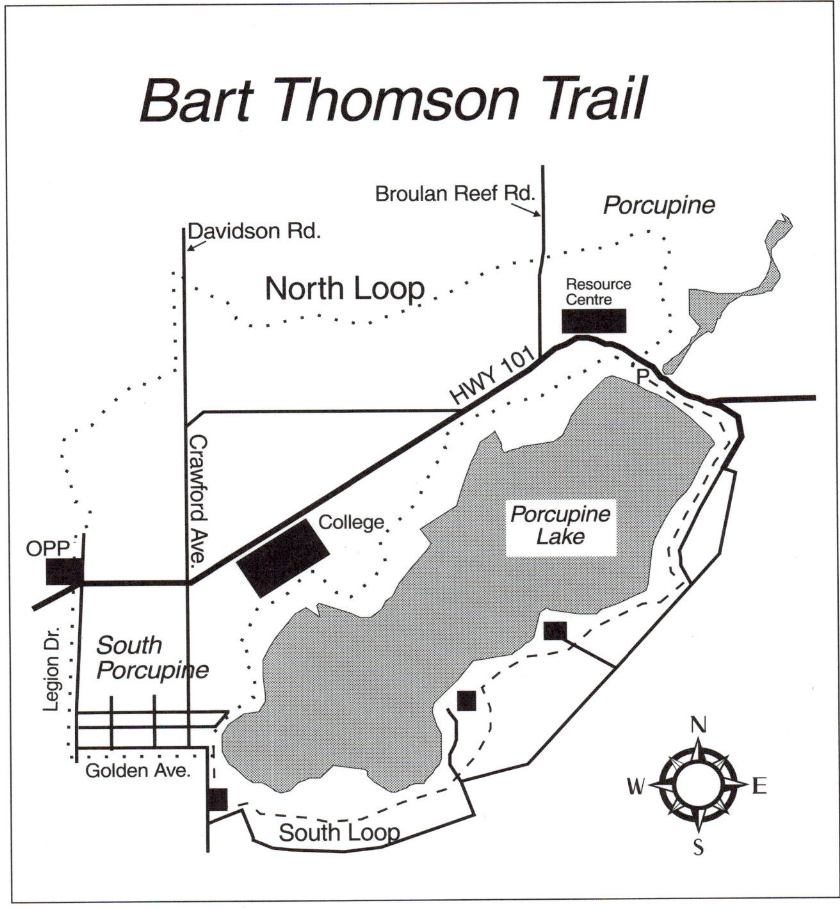

7 trails: 39 km

Location:

This conservation area is located at 5th Line and Landslide Road in Sault Ste. Marie. Follow Highway 17 north until you reach 6th Line. Follow 6th Line until you reach Landslide Road and then turn south (right) and follow the road until you reach the parking lot at Hiawatha Lodge.

Rating: Moderate/Difficult

The Trails

All the trails radiate from the beautiful Hiawatha Lodge. The lodge is built from hand-hewn logs and it is the perfect spot to relax after a hard ride. All the trails offer excellent scenery and should challenge even the most experienced mountain biker. As well, these trails are only minutes away from downtown Sault Ste. Marie. Now that I have told you where these great trails are, I will let you explore the trails on your own! The trail lengths are as follows:

Red Pine Trail:	10 km
Lookout Trail:	7 km
Pinder Farm Trail:	5 km
Kinsman Trail:	2 km
Crystal Creek Trail:	5 km
Hiawatha Trail:	7.5 km
Olympic Trail:	2.5 km

Camping

Bell's Point Beach (705) 759-1561
Sault Ste. Marie KOA (705) 759-2344
Trout Lake Resort (705) 777-2382

Hotels/Resorts

Journey's End Motel (705) 759-8000
Norwest Motel and Inn (705) 942-1970
Water Tower Inn (705) 949-8111

For more information contact:

Sault Ste. Marie Region Conservation Authority
Civic Centre
99 Foster Drive
Sault Ste. Marie, Ontario
P6A 5X6
(705) 759-5341

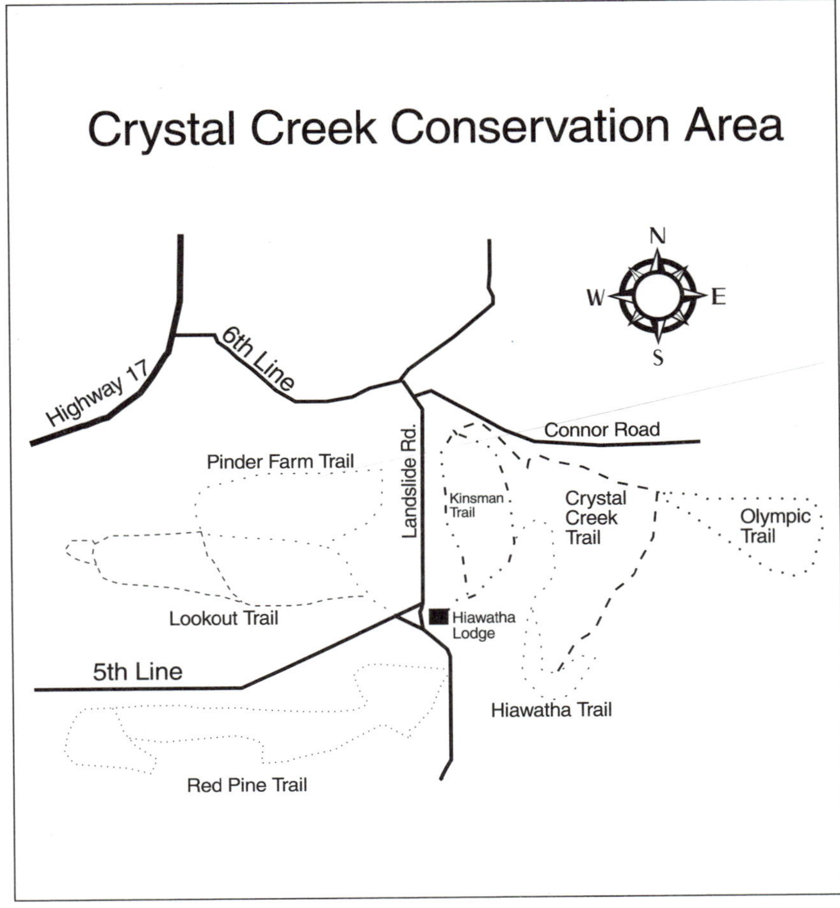

Fort Creek Conservation Area, Sault Ste. Marie

5 trails: 8 km

Location:

In the centre of Sault Ste. Marie on Highway 550. Enter the conservation area from Highway 550 and park in the lot provided.

Rating: Easy/Moderate

The Trails

The conservation area is spread over 73 hectares and has five excellent mountain-biking trails. The scenery on these trails is spectacular. You can take in the beautiful boreal forest and the St. Lawrence lowland forest. The flora and fauna in this conservation area are very fragile, so be careful not to leave the marked trails. Watch out for beaver at the north end of the conservation area. The boreal forest area can be found on the north-facing slopes of the conservation area. I hope you enjoy this interesting location.

Camping

Bell's Point Beach (705) 759-1561
Sault Ste. Marie KOA (705) 759-2344
Trout Lake Resort (705) 777-2382

Hotels/Resorts

Algoma Cabins and Motel (705) 256-8681
Journey's End Motel (705) 759-8000
Water Tower Inn (705) 949-8111

For more information contact:

Sault Ste. Marie Region Conservation Authority
Civic Centre
99 Foster Drive
Sault Ste. Marie, Ontario
P6A 5X6
(705) 759-5341

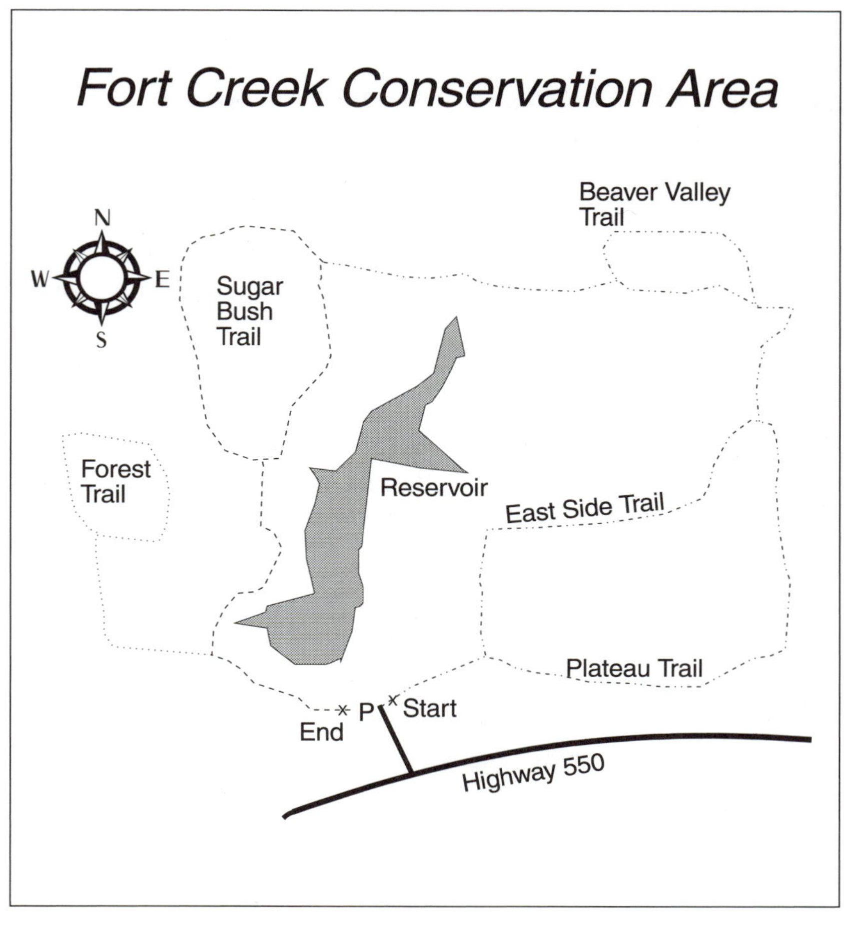
Fort Creek Conservation Area
N
W
E
S
Beaver Valley Trail
Sugar Bush Trail
Forest Trail
Reservoir
East Side Trail
Plateau Trail
End
P
Start
Highway 550

Golden Springs Trail, Timmins

1 trail: 18 km

Location:

This trail is found just off Highway 655 northeast of Timmins. Access can be gained from Schumacher Park and other points just off Highway 655 (see map).

Rating: Easy/Moderate

Golden Springs Trail: 8 km

The crushed-rock trail is ideal for mountain biking and it is well marked. This trail begins in Schumacher Park and continues north up to Hersey Lake Conservation Area. The trail crosses the old Hollinger bucket line (used to move gravel) and winds its way to the northeast across a large tailings area.

At this point the trail strikes northward for approximately 1 kilometre until it reaches an access road, which it follows eastward for several hundred metres. A sign marks the entrance to the trail, which then leads north to the Hersey Lake Conservation Area.

The causeway marks the southern boundary of the conservation area and it is from here that the trail starts to wind through jack pine forest. After crossing the Hersey Lake access road (which emerges at Manitoulin Transport on Highway 655) the trail dips through several deep gullies.

The final leg consists of an old forest access road that loops around a small lake at the far north end of the conservation area. Turn around and ride back down to the start of the trail at Schumacher Park.

Camping

Horseshoe Lake Park (705) 268-2033
Kettle Lake Provincial Park (705) 267-7951

Hotels/Resorts

Journey's End Motel (705) 264-9474
Senator Hotel (705) 267-6211
Travelway Inn (705) 360-1122

For more information contact:

Mattagami Region Conservation Authority
Civic Centre
133 Cedar Street South
Timmins, Ontario
P4N 2G9
(705) 264-5309

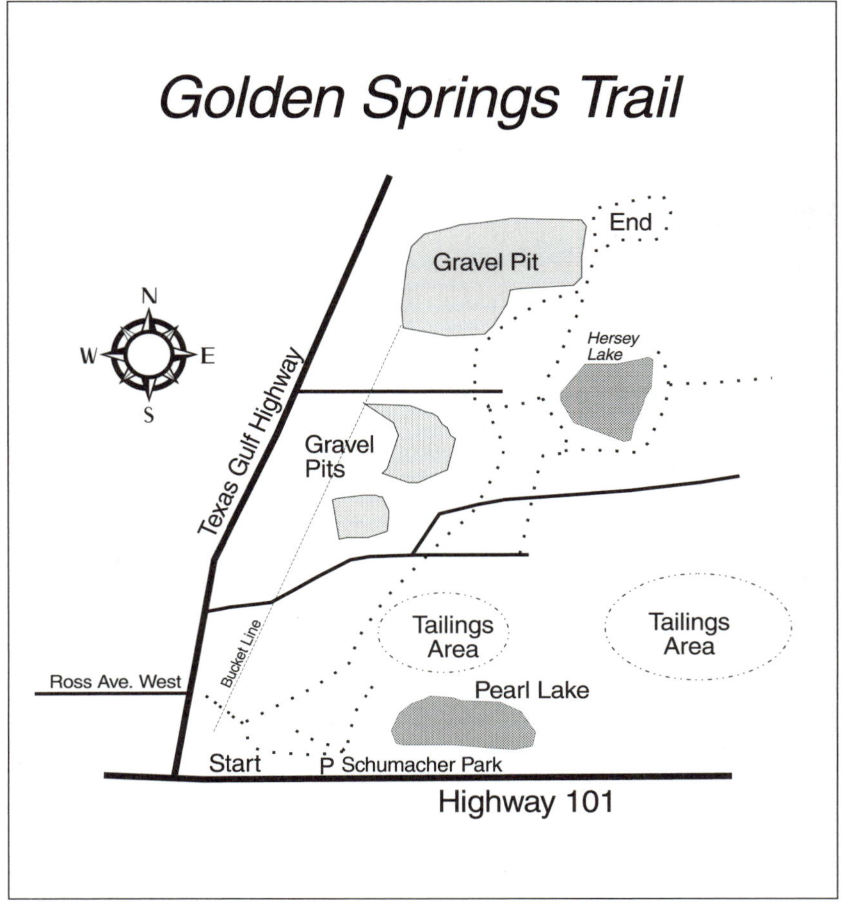

3 trails: 8.5 km

Location:

The Hersey Lake Conservation Area is located off Highway 655 northeast of Timmins. Follow Highway 655 north until you reach the access road to the conservation area. Follow the access road for approximately 1 kilometre until you reach the parking lot.

Rating: Easy/Moderate

Tamarack Nature Trail: 1.5 km

This self-guided trail starts near the parking lot and passes through a variety of natural areas typical of the northern environment. There are fifteen interpretive stations along this trail. Each station is marked with a post that describes the unique physical, biological, and historical features of the area. Lookout points and benches are provided, so you can stop and enjoy a beautiful view of the surrounding countryside.

Hersey Lake Fitness Trail: 2 km

This trail takes you around the perimeter of Hersey Lake. There are ten exercise stations positioned on this trail to give you an extra workout.

Golden Springs Loop: 5 km

This trail allows the mountain biker to travel to every corner of the conservation area. There are a number of rest stops and lookouts along this trail to make your ride more enjoyable.

I hope you enjoy these three great trails.

Camping

Horseshoe Lake Park (705) 268-2033
Kettle Lake Provincial Park (705) 267-7951

Hotels/Resorts

Journey's End Motel (705) 264-9474
Senator Hotel (705) 267-6211
Travelway Inn (705) 360-1122

For more information contact:

Mattagami Region Conservation Authority
Civic Centre
133 Cedar Street South
Timmins, Ontario
P4N 2G9
(705) 264-5309

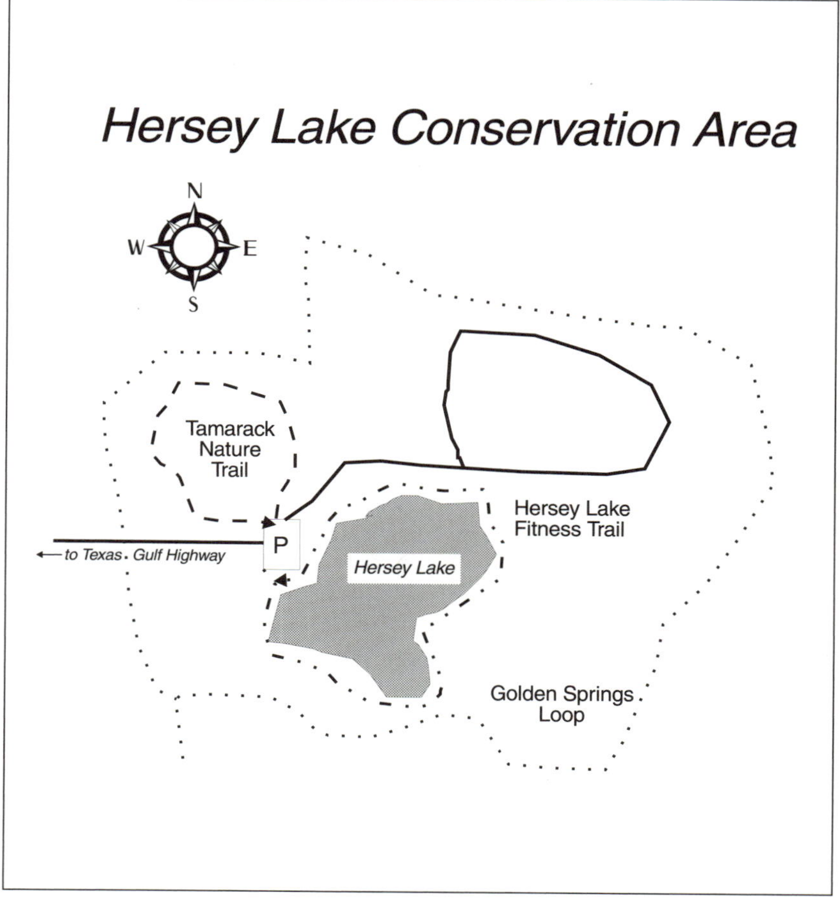

4 trails: 43 km

Location:

The park is located 25 kilometres north of Elliot Lake on Highway 639. A parking lot is provided at the park entrance.

Rating: Moderate/Difficult

Christman Cross-Country Ski Trail: 11 km

To access this trail, follow the main park road down the hill, past the gatehouse and the entrance road, to the park office. Turn right at the sign and trail brochure box that marks this junction. The trail follows the waterline for a short distance, then turns north (left) across an open area. After crossing the main road, the trail runs through rolling hardwood forest for the next kilometre.

You will now turn east along an old logging road and begin a slight descent, which leads into a fairly steep hill. The trail turns north, then west, around the end of Helenbar Lake. After crossing a small creek draining into Helenbar Lake, you begin climbing a series of hills. A rest area is provided at the top. Continue on the trail until it ends at the main park road.

Helenbar Lake Trail: 7 km

This trail starts at the end of the main park access road and runs south of Helenbar Lake and then north of Semiwite Lake. This is an excellent trail for beginners. There is a scenic lookout halfway along this trail that provides an excellent view of the surrounding area.

Semiwite Lake Trail: 12 km

This trail begins a short way down the main park access road. The trail is a 12-kilometre loop around Semiwite Lake that includes many historic sites, such as an old cabin and a geologic fault line.

Cobra Lake Trail: 11 km

This trail is located 11 kilometres north of the main park entrance. It is a highly scenic trail that leads you past the remains of old copper mines and a stand of old-growth white and red pine. Near the end of the trail there is a series of lookouts that affords an unequalled view of the surrounding area. It is the perfect spot for a rest stop.

Camping

Mississagi Provincial Park (705) 848-2806

Hotels/Resorts

Laurentian Lodge (705) 848-0423
Wilderness Lodge (705) 848-2843

For more information contact:

Mississagi Provincial Park Superintendent
P.O. Box 150, 62 Queen Avenue
Blind River, Ontario P0R 1B0 (705) 356-2234

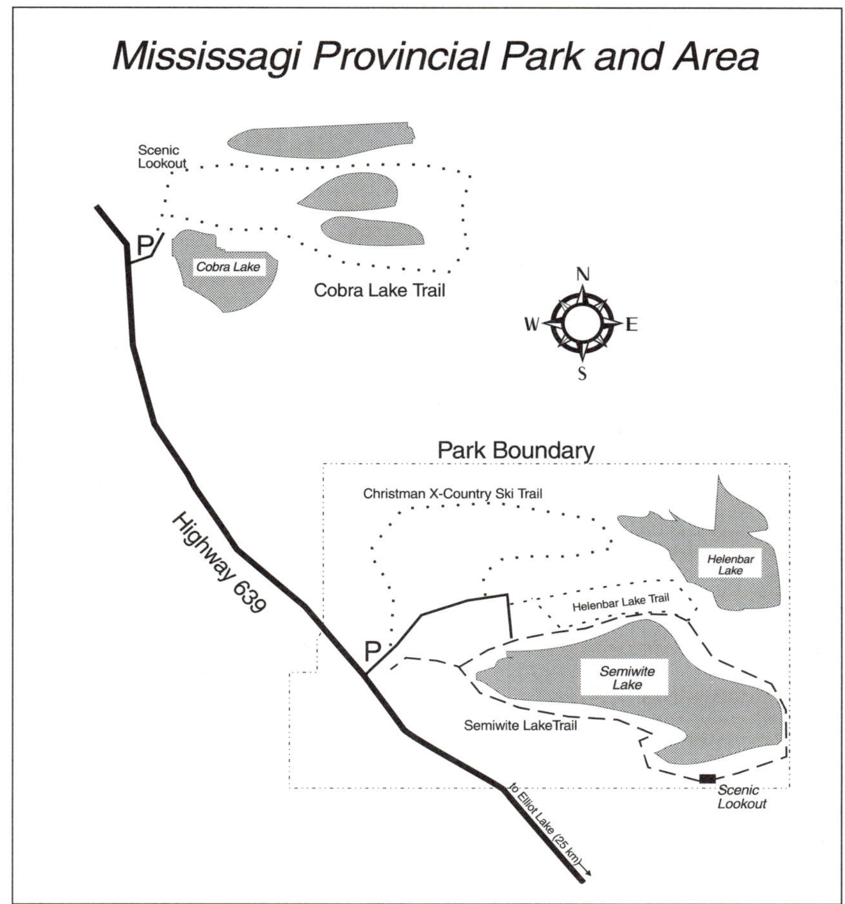

2 trails: 4 km ↔

Location:

This conservation area is located off Highway 550, on Lake Superior, the junction of Sunnyside Beach Road and Walls Road, within the city limits of Sault Ste. Marie.

Rating: Easy

Upper Indian Ridge Trail: 2 km

The Upper Indian Ridge Trail is situated on an escarpment in a hardwood forest. This trail presents a striking view of Lake Superior.

Beaver Trail: 2 km

The Beaver Trail is located on a beach terrace surrounded by a marsh. The plants located on this trail include the rare pitcher plant. If you're lucky you may share the trail with a moose. (You may want to yield the right of way!)

Camping

Bell's Point Beach (705) 759-1561
Sault Ste. Marie KOA (705) 759-2344
Trout Lake Resort (705) 777-2382

Hotels/Resorts

Algoma Cabins and Motel (705) 256-8681
Journey's End Motel (705) 759-8000
Water Tower Inn (705) 949-8111

For more information contact:

Sault Ste. Marie Region Conservation Authority
Civic Centre
99 Foster Drive
Sault Ste. Marie, Ontario
P6A 5X6
(705) 759-5341

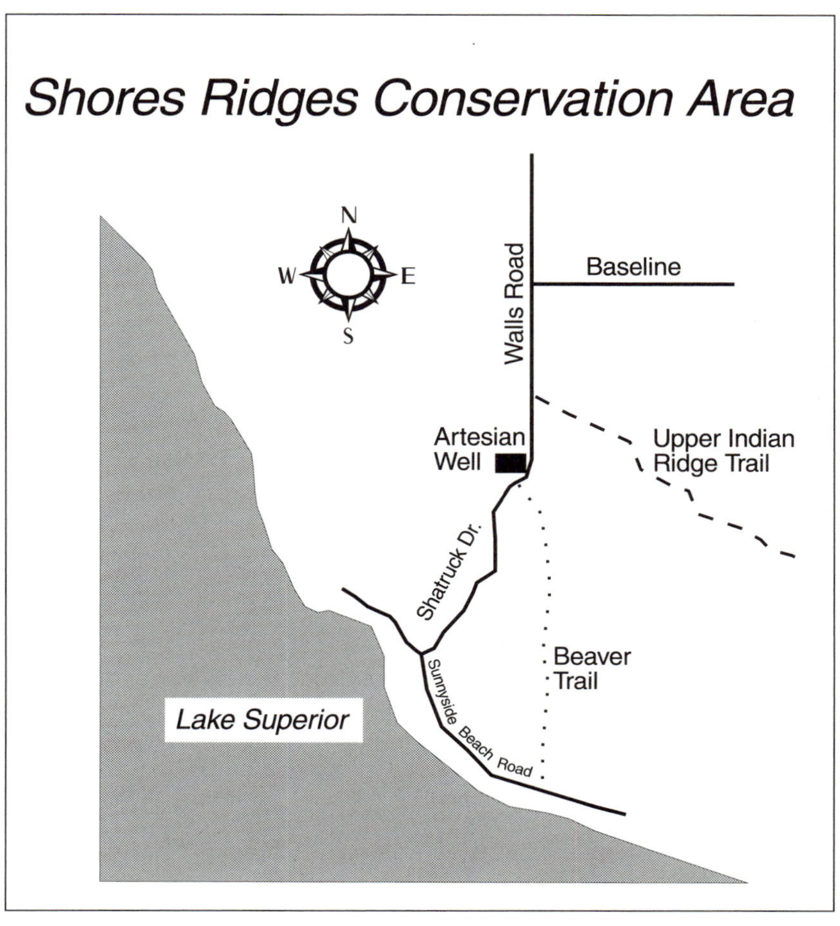

Shores Ridges Conservation Area
N
W
E
S
Walls Road
Baseline
Artesian Well
Upper Indian Ridge Trail
Shatruck Dr.
Beaver Trail
Sunnyside Beach Road
Lake Superior

3 trails: 63 km

Location:

This provincial park is located 56 kilometres from Thunder Bay. Follow Highway 11/17 from Thunder Bay for 42 kilometres, then follow Highway 587 for 14 kilometres to the park entrance.

Rating: Moderate

The park was originally established in 1944 as Sibley Provincial Park. The name was changed in 1988 to Sleeping Giant Provincial Park. The eastern lowlands of the park rise gently from Lake Superior, while the western shore is dominated by huge cliffs over 240 metres high. The park's terrain is characterized by deep valleys, sheer cliffs and clear, fast-running streams. It is not unusual to see white-tailed deer, red fox, porcupine, moose and even bears in the park. The larger animals should be treated with caution.

North Gravel Road Trail: 21 km

The North Gravel Road Trail begins at the Rita Lake gatehouse and travels 21 kilometres on a gravel road to the Bay's End picnic area and lookout. Stop at the Thunder Bay and Caribou Island lookouts while on this trail.

South Gravel Road Trail: 16 km

This trail begins at the north junction of the gravel road and Highway 587. Follow the gravel road south around Marie Louise Lake. Ride past the park office and head north. The gravel road meets up with Highway 587. Follow the highway for a few kilometres to where you parked your car.

Highway 587 Trail: 26 km

This trail follows Highway 587 the length of the provincial park. Be careful on this trail, since it is a highway.

Camping

Happyland Campground (807) 473-9003
Sleeping Giant Provincial Park (807) 475-1531
Thunder Bay KOA (807) 683-6221

Hotels/Resorts

Best Western (807) 577-4241
Landmark Inn (807) 767-1681
Valhalla Inn (807) 577-1121

For more information contact:

Superintendent
Sleeping Giant Provincial Park
Pass Lake, Ontario
P0T 2M0
(807) 475-1531

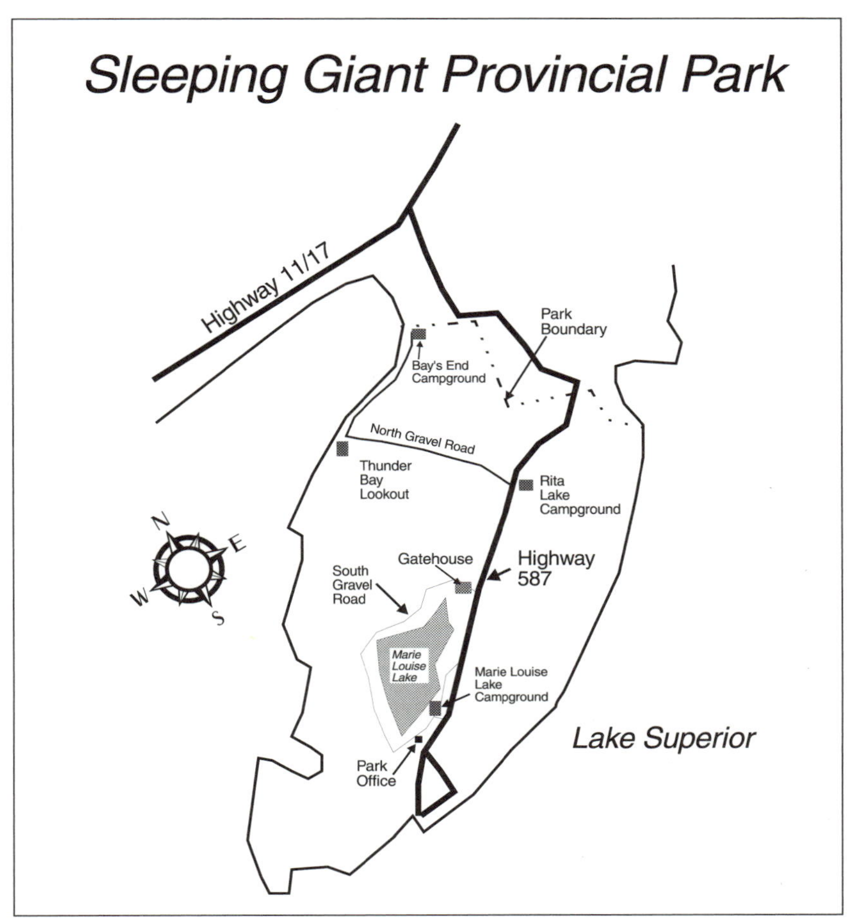

Southeast Region Trails

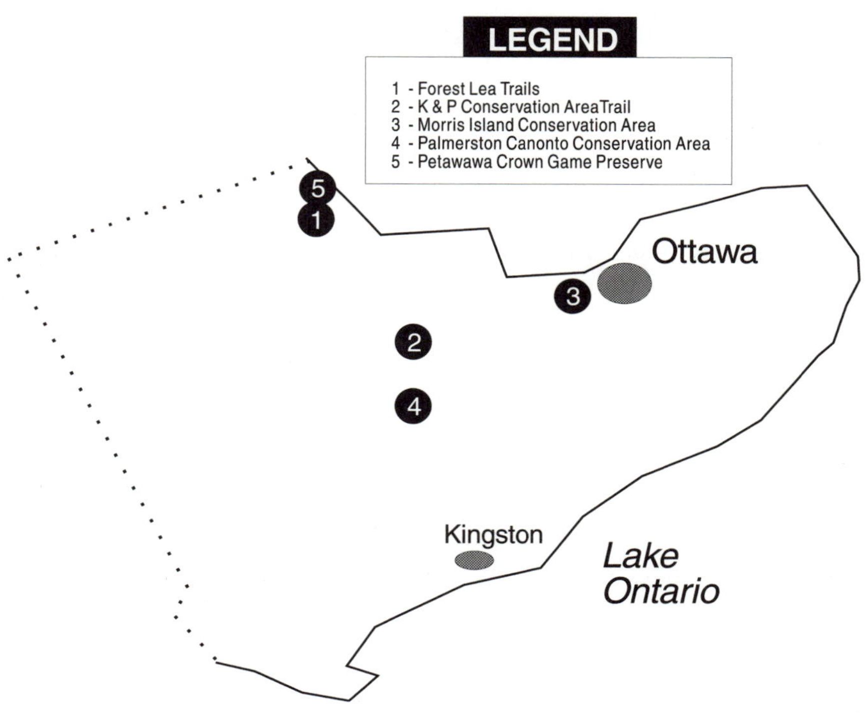

5 trails: 11 km

Location:

The Forest Lea Trails are located on the Forest Lea Road (Alice Twp. Road No. 14) 13 kilometres west of Pembroke and are maintained by the Ontario Ministry of Natural Resources.

Rating: Moderate/Difficult

Ruffed Grouse Trail: 2.7 km

This trail begins at the parking lot and travels through a variety of forest types for 2.7 kilometres, eventually returning to the parking lot. The terrain is gently rolling or flat except for a downhill ride that starts in the plantation just beyond trail marker number seven. The trail provides the novice mountain biker with a number of short but challenging uphill climbs.

Tall Pine Trail: 2.2 km

This trail begins at trail marker number one and travels 2.2 kilometres to the junction with the Ruffed Grouse Trail at trail marker number seven. Designed for the intermediate mountain biker, this trail crosses slightly rougher terrain, with a number of uphill climbs and a few quick, short downhill rides.

Poplar Grove: 1.4 km

This intermediate trail begins at trail marker number two on the Tall Pine Trail and terminates at trail marker number four on the Beaver Ridge loop. This 1.4-kilometre trail provides the mountain biker with gradual downhill rides.

Beaver Ridge: 2.1 km

Access to the Beaver Ridge Trail can be obtained from either the Tall Pine Trail at trail marker number three or the Poplar Grove Trail at trail marker number four. This trail is designed for the advanced mountain biker and features quick downhill rides combined with a long uphill climb.

Lookout Ridge Trail: 2.8 km

The Lookout Ridge Trail begins at trail marker number five on the Beaver Ridge loop and travels a total distance of 2.8 kilometres to its intersection with Tall Pine Trail at trail marker number six. This trail is for the advanced mountain biker. Lookout Ridge Trail combines a number of short downhill rides with several long uphill climbs. I highly recommend this trail.

Camping

Riverside Park (613) 735-2251

Hotels/Resorts

Days Inn (613) 735-6868

For more information contact:

Ministry of Natural Resources
Box 220, Riverside Drive
Pembroke, Ontario N4K 3E4
(613) 732-3661

K and P Conservation Area Trail, Barryvale

1 trail: 80 km ↔

Location:

Parking is available in Barryvale, off Highway 511, and at Lavant Station, and at Highway 509 near Snow Station Road.

Rating: Moderate/Difficult (due to its length)

K and P Trail

This conservation area was formerly part of the rail line between Kingston and Pembroke. Since 1972, the right of way between Highway 509 (near Snowdown Road) and Barryvale has been used as a recreational trail. During the spring, summer and fall the conservation area provides a scenic route for hikers, cyclists, horseback riders and ATV users.

This 80-kilometre round-trip trail is excellent for mountain bikers who enjoy a relatively easy but long trail. The trail begins in Barryvale and continues south along an old railway right of way. There are numerous lakes, wetlands and scenic locations along the trail. Shelters, fire pits and privies are provided on the way. You should definitely ride this trail at least once in your lifetime.

Camping

Bon Echo Provincial Park (613) 336-2228
Sharbot Lake Provincial Park (613) 335-2814
Silver Lake Provincial Park (613) 268-2000

Hotels/Resorts

Days Inn Valley Motel (613) 432-3636
Palmerston Motel (613) 479-2888
Trout Lake Hotel (613) 479-2987

For more information contact:

Manager
Mississippi Valley Conservation Authority
P.O. Box 268,
Lanark, Ontario
N4K 3E4
(613) 259-2421

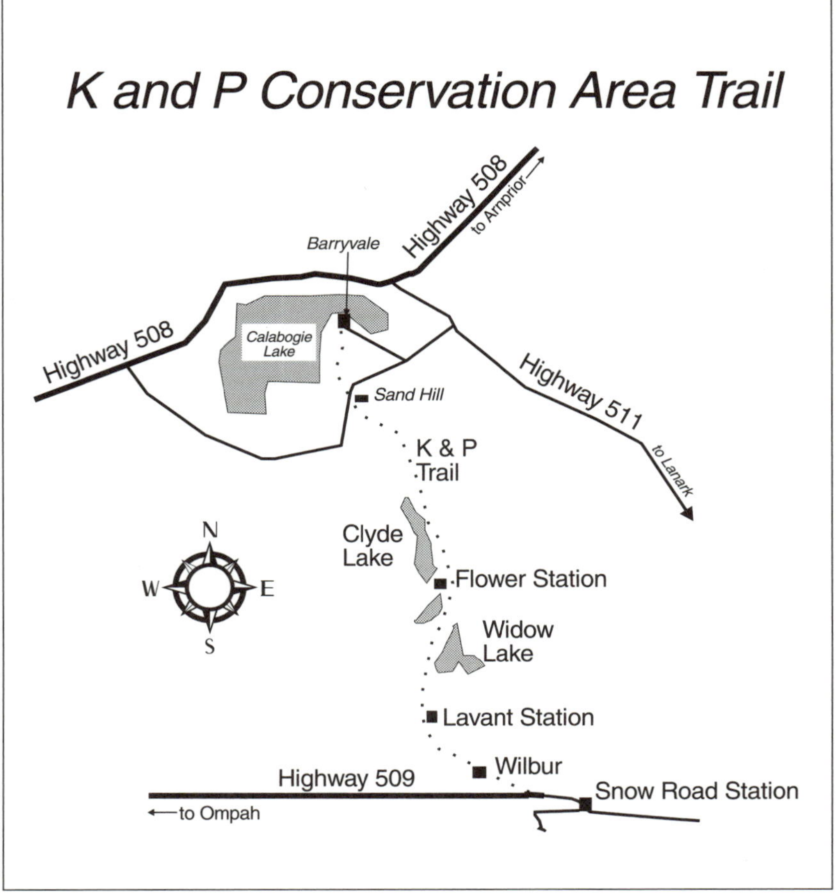

3 trails: 13 km

Location:

Along the Ottawa River near the community of Fitzroy Harbour, northwest of Ottawa. Follow Regional Road 22 northeast from Fitzroy Harbour. Turn left at Logger's Way and follow this road until you reach Kingdon Road. Turn right at Kingdon Road and continue until you reach the conservation area.

Rating: Moderate

North Trail: 3 km

The North Trail starts at the parking lot at the west side of the conservation area. Follow the trail across the peninsula and across a bridge to an island. The trail turns south and heads back to the parking lot. There are numerous benches from which to view the scenery. Watch for deer, beaver, porcupine and squirrels on your ride. The trails in this conservation area offer a challenging ride for most mountain bikers.

Central Trail: 4 km ↔

The Central Trail starts at the end of the access road into the conservation area. Follow the trail straight east over the Ottawa River on the causeway. The trail ends at the edge of the conservation area. Turn around and head west and back to the parking lot. You can get an excellent view of the Ottawa River on the causeway. There are benches and washrooms along the way.

South Trail: 6 km

The South Trail starts off on the east side of the causeway on the Central Trail. Follow this trail east along the Ottawa River and then north through the small islands. This trail has many side branches and loops, which you should explore on your ride (see map).

Camping

Fitzroy Provincial Park (613) 623-5159
Fraser's Campground (613) 623-3872

Hotels/Resorts

Country Squire Motel (613) 623-6556
Twin Maples Motel R.P.G. (613) 623-4271
Vacation Inns (613) 623-7991

For more information contact:

Manager
Mississippi Valley Conservation Authority
P.O. Box 268
Lanark, Ontario
N4K 3E4
(613) 259-2421

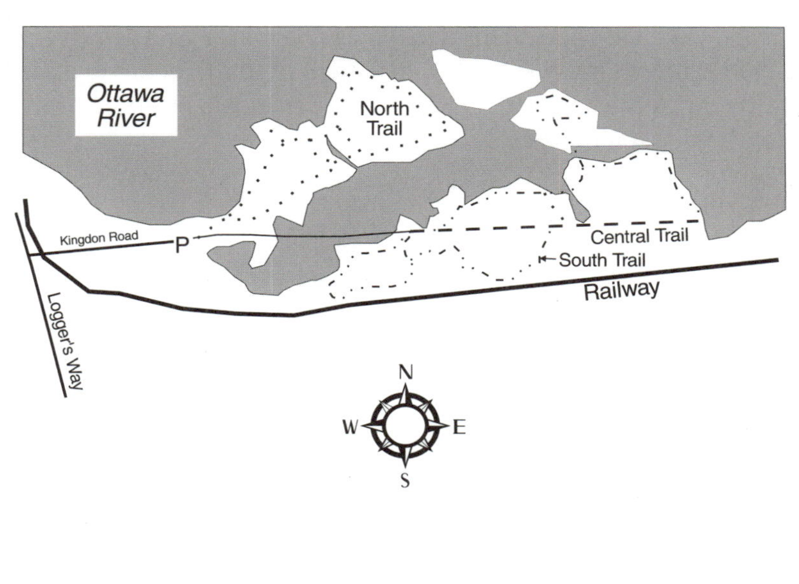

Palmerston Canonto Conservation Area, Ompah

1 trail: 6 km

Location:

At the junction of Palmerston and Canonto lakes, approximately 3.5 kilometres east of Ompah off Highway 509. It is open to the public year-round.

Rating: Difficult

The Palmerston Canonto Conservation Area provides a unique combination of conservation, nature appreciation and recreational opportunities. It contains a wide variety of natural areas: deciduous and coniferous forests, beaver ponds, small streams, spectacular rock lookouts, and a waterfront park with a bench.

Main Trail: 6 km

Parts of this trail are very difficult and should only be attempted by advanced mountain bikers. Start riding the trail north from the parking lot up the side of Canonto Lake. The trail turns west and then south after a short way. The trail then loops back west and finally turns north. Follow the trail to its end in the swamp and turn around and come back.

You will have the opportunity to stop at several lookout points along the ride. I recommend you take advantage of these lookouts to get a better view of the beautiful countryside. Bring some food and lots of water for this tough ride.

Camping

Bon Echo Provincial Park (613) 336-2228
Sharbot Lake Provincial Park (613) 335-2814
Silver Lake Provincial Park (613) 268-2000

Hotels/Resorts

Friendship Inn, Perth (613) 267-3300
Palmerston Motel (613) 479-2888
Trout Lake Hotel (613) 479-2987

For more information contact:

Manager
Mississippi Valley Conservation Authority
P.O. Box 268
Lanark, Ontario
N4K 3E4
(613) 259-2421

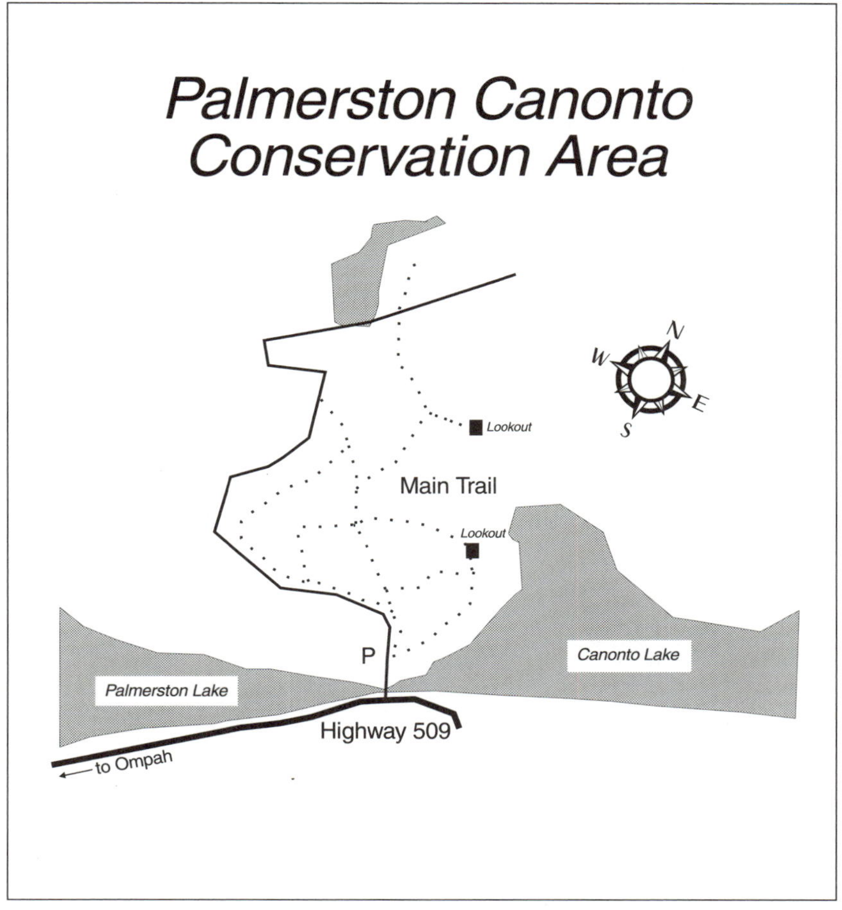

2 trails: 6.6 km

Location:

The Petawawa Crown Game Preserve trails are located off Laurentian Drive (old Highway 17) in Petawawa Township, on the property commonly known as the Petawawa Fish Hatchery.

Orange Loop Trail: 4.4 km

This trail extends 4.4 kilometres from the parking lot at the base of the Petawawa Terrace out towards the Ottawa River and then circles back to the parking lot. For something different, ride up the road to the fish hatchery and have a look around.

Green Loop Trail: 2.3 km

This trail begins at the parking lot located at the entrance to the property and continues 2.3 kilometres along the top of the Petawawa Terrace, terminating at the parking lot where you started.

Camping

Pine Ridge Park and Resort (613) 732-9891
Riverside Park (613) 735-2251
White Sands Trailer Park (613) 582-3840

Hotels/Resorts

Days Inn (613) 735-6868
Forest Lea Inn (613) 732-9981
Journey's End Motel (613) 735-1057

For more information contact:

District Manager
Ministry of Natural Resources
Box 220, Riverside Drive
Pembroke, Ontario
N4K 3E4
(613) 732-3661

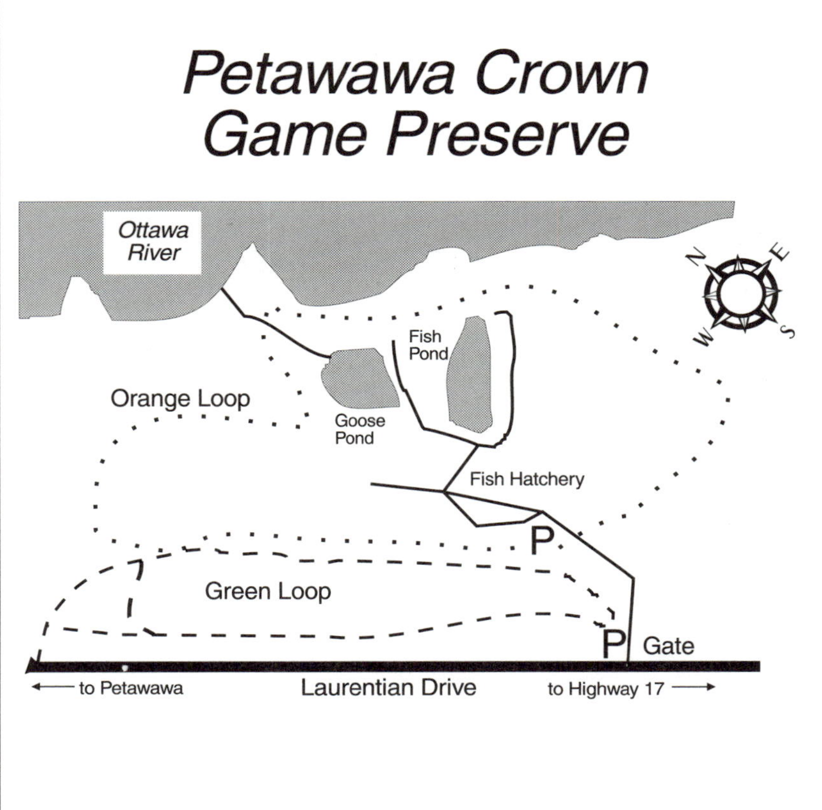
Petawawa Crown
Game Preserve
Ottawa
River
N
E
W
S
Fish
Pond
Orange Loop
Goose
Pond
Fish Hatchery
P
Green Loop
P
Gate
to Petawawa
Laurentian Drive
to Highway 17

Southwest Region Trails

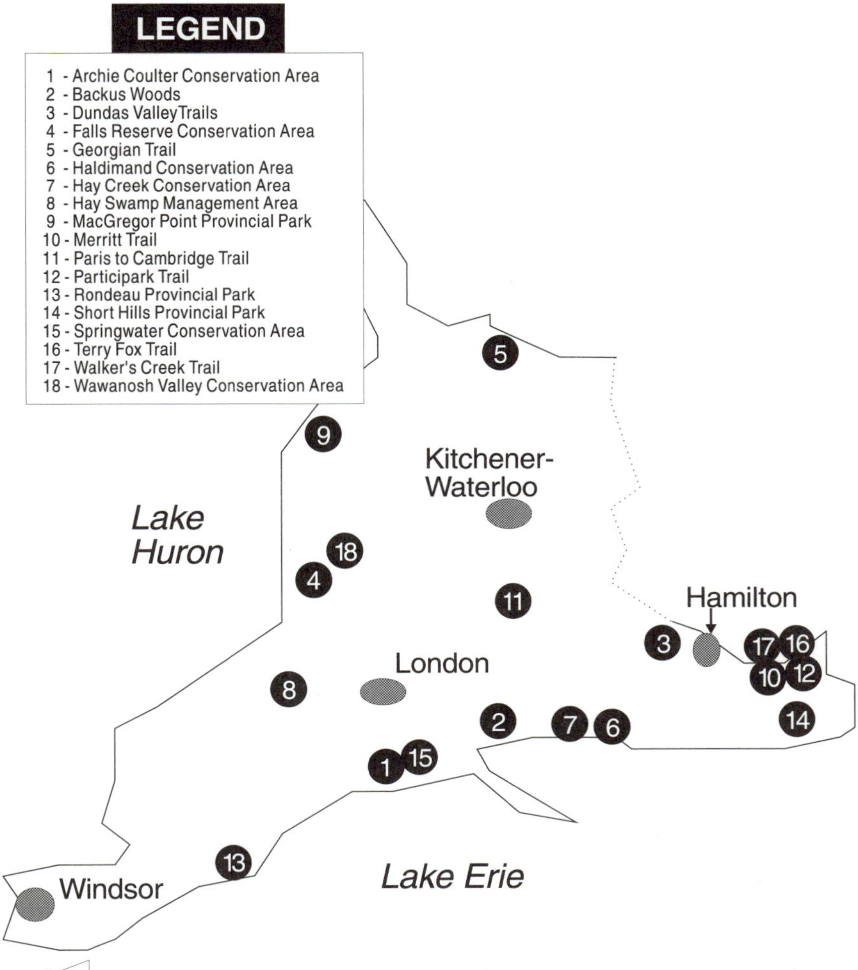

LEGEND

1 - Archie Coulter Conservation Area
2 - Backus Woods
3 - Dundas ValleyTrails
4 - Falls Reserve Conservation Area
5 - Georgian Trail
6 - Haldimand Conservation Area
7 - Hay Creek Conservation Area
8 - Hay Swamp Management Area
9 - MacGregor Point Provincial Park
10 - Merritt Trail
11 - Paris to Cambridge Trail
12 - Participark Trail
13 - Rondeau Provincial Park
14 - Short Hills Provincial Park
15 - Springwater Conservation Area
16 - Terry Fox Trail
17 - Walker's Creek Trail
18 - Wawanosh Valley Conservation Area

Kitchener-Waterloo

Lake Huron

Hamilton

London

Windsor

Lake Erie

4 km of trails

Location:

The Archie Coulter Conservation Area is located off 7th Concession. Take Highway 74 south from Highway 401 at Exit 195. Follow Highway 74 south until you reach Highway 3. Follow Highway 3 west until you reach County Road 36. Follow this road south until you come to 7th Concession. Follow 7th Concession east until you reach the conservation area.

Rating: Easy

The Trails

The trail starts at the parking lot just off 7th Concession. This 54-hectare conservation area has a beautiful Carolinian forest containing black walnut, sycamore, eastern cottonwood and black oak. You can also view thirty-five species of birds, including the red-eyed vireo, indigo bunting and the great blue heron. You will want to climb the observation tower at the north end of the conservation area to have a look around. Who knows, you may even catch a glimpse of a white-tailed deer or a rare indigo bunting.

Camping

Dalewood Conservation Area (519) 631-1270
London KOA (519) 644-0222
Port Burwell Provincial Park (519) 874-4691

Hotels/Resorts

Cardinal Court Motel (519) 633-0740
Covey Bros. Motel and Family Restaurant (519) 842-7366
Journey's End Motel (519) 633-4082

For more information contact:

Manager
Catfish Creek Conservation Authority
R.R. 5
Aylmer, Ontario
N5H 2R4
(519) 773-9037

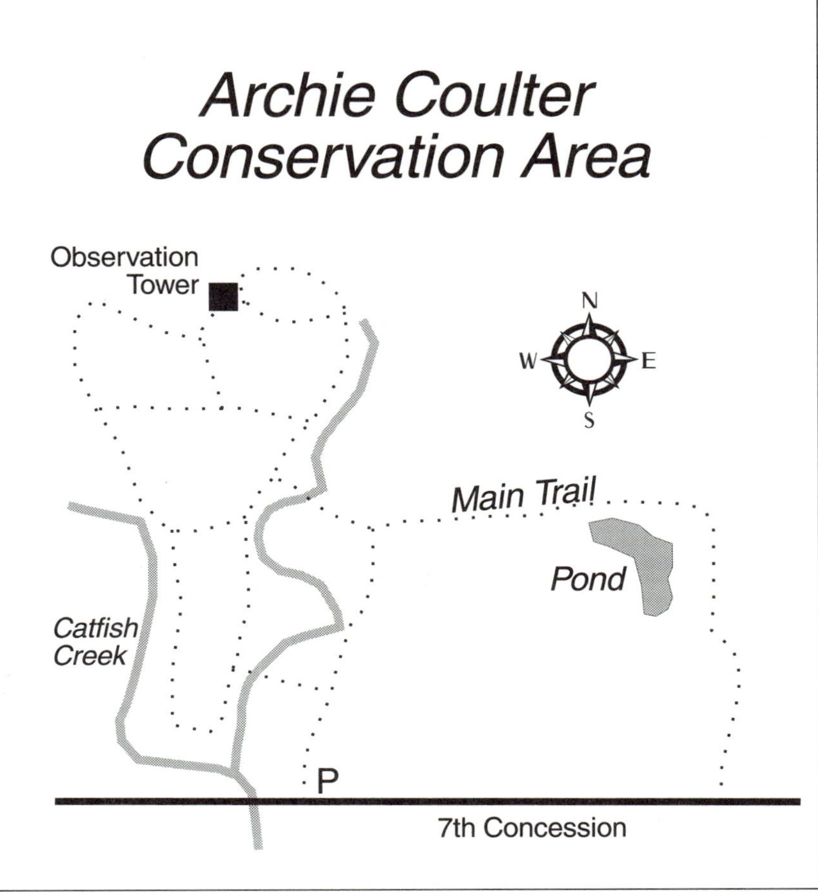

3 trails: 13 km

Location:

Access to the Backus Woods trails is off Highway 24 north of Port Rowan. You should park your car in the lot provided.

Rating: Moderate

Wetlands Trail: 6 km

This trail starts off at the north parking lot. Follow the trail south across 4th Concession. The trail loops north and crosses 4th Concession again. The trail returns you to the trail you started on and eventually to the starting point. You will see numerous plants and animals on this trail. Backus Woods is one of the largest forest tracts remaining in southwestern Ontario. Lake Erie moderates the climate of this region and many plants and animals that are usually found much further south can be found here. Watch for southern tree species such as tulip-tree, black gum, sweet chestnut and swamp white oak.

Sugar Bush Trail: 4 km

This trail starts at the 4th Concession where the Wetlands Trail crosses it. Follow the trail south and then east. The trail follows an access road for a short distance and then becomes a dirt trail again. The trail joins another access road for short distance as it heads north. Leave the road and head east along the dirt trail. The trail eventually loops back westward, crossing the access road several times before you return to the start.

Flood Plain Trail: 3 km ↔

This trail starts where the Sugar Bush Trail loops westward. Follow this trail south along Dedrich Creek and past the 3rd Concession. The trail ends a short way beyond the 3rd Concession. You can turn around and head north. Keep a lookout for opossum on this trail.

Camping

Backus Heritage Conservation Area (905) 586-2201
Haldimand Conservation Area (905) 776-2700
Selkirk Provincial Park (905) 776-2600

Hotels/Resorts

Brant Hill Inn (519) 583-1501
Bucks Cottages (519) 583-2263
Erie Beach Hotel (519) 583-1391

For more information contact:

Manager
Long Point Region Conservation Authority
R.R. 3
Simcoe, Ontario
N3Y 4K2
(519) 428-4623

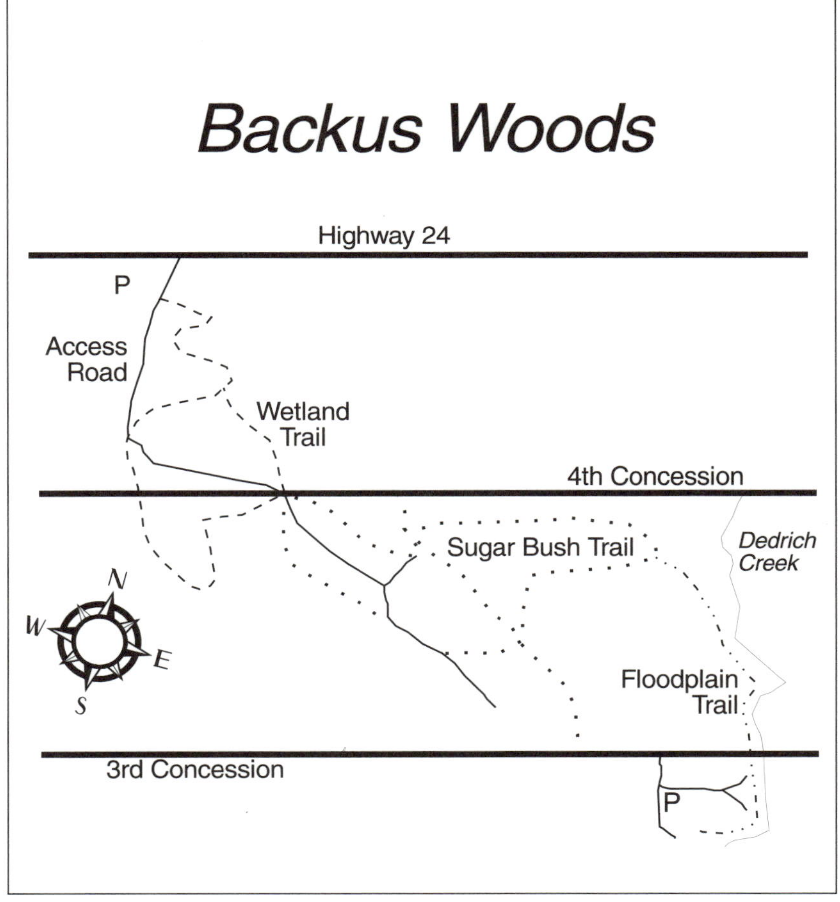

22 trails: 41 km

Location:

Access to the Dundas Valley trails is off Governors Road in Ancaster, just west of Hamilton.

Rating: Moderate/Difficult

The Trails

There are no trail maps included in this guide for the Dundas Valley because the trail system is very complex and the Hamilton Region Conservation Authority has produced an excellent trail map of the Dundas Valley. You should send away for this map before you visit the valley. (The address is provided at the end of this trail description.) I would also recommend a good map of the Hamilton–Ancaster area.

The Hamilton Region Conservation Authority began the construction of these trails in 1976. The forty-one trails pass through 1,000 hectares of thick forest, field, marsh and stream valley, and offer hours of enjoyment to those who appreciate beautiful scenery. There are many rare and wonderful animals and plants.

Ride carefully and cautiously because the trails will be crowded with hikers and other mountain bikers. Stay off the trails when they are wet in April and early May, so that trail damage will be kept to a minimum.

Camping

Confederation Park Campground (905) 578-1644
Valens Conservation Area (905) 659-7715

Hotels/Resorts

Journey's End Motel (905) 560-4500
Quality Inn (905) 528-0611
Sheraton Hamilton Hotel (905) 529-5515

For more information contact:

Hamilton Region Conservation Authority
P.O. Box 7099
838 Mineral Springs Road
Ancaster, Ontario
L9G 3L3
(905) 525-2181

Trail guides are available for $2.75.

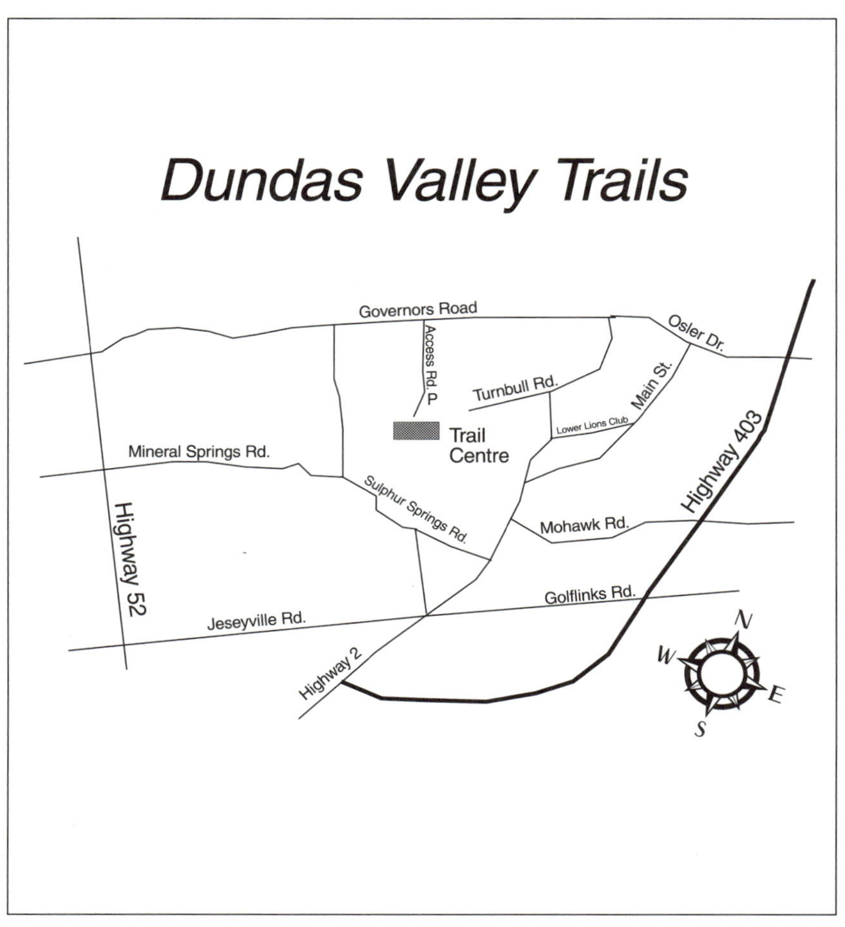

1 trail: 3 km ↔

Location:

The Falls Reserve Conservation Area is located off County Road 31 near the town of Goderich.

Rating: Easy

Falls Reserve Trail: 3 km

Park your car in the parking lot just past the fish pond. Ride your bike approximately 300 metres to the start of the trail. The trail follows the Maitland River west and then north until it meets up with the main park access road. Ride down the trail again or ride on the access road until you reach the parking lot.

You can head over to the swimming area and spend a few hours relaxing in the sun. You can also try riding around some of the campground roads, but watch for cars! The conservation area is open year-round for day-use activities such as mountain biking.

Camping

Falls Reserve Conservation Area (519) 524-6429
Lake Huron Resort (519) 524-6438
Shelter Valley Trailer Park (519) 524-4141

Hotels/Resorts

Benmiller Inn (519) 524-2191
Cedar Lodge Motel (519) 524-8379
Maple Leaf Motel (519) 524-2302

For more information contact:

Communications Co-ordinator
Maitland Valley Conservation Area
P.O. Box 127
Wroxeter, Ontario
N0G 2X0
(519) 335-3557

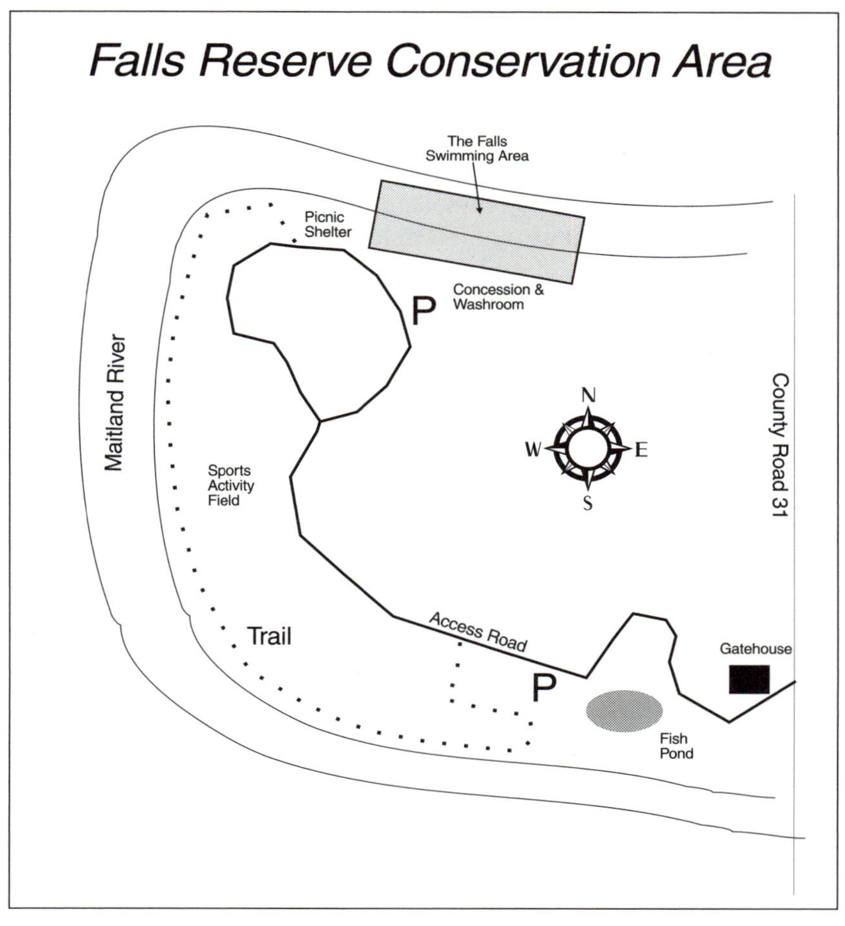
Falls Reserve Conservation Area
The Falls
Swimming Area
Picnic
Shelter
Concession &
Washroom
P
Maitland River
N
W
E
S
County Road 31
Sports
Activity
Field
Trail
Access Road
P
Gatehouse
Fish
Pond

1 trail: 64 km ↔

Location:

The beginning of this trail is on St. Vincent Street in the town of Meaford.

Rating: Moderate/Difficult (due to its length)

Georgian Trail

The trail begins on St. Vincent Street in Meaford. Follow the trail for about 4 kilometres until you reach the Grey County Forest. Slow down and see if you can spot some wildlife here. Continue on the trail for another 2 kilometres and you will come to the Christie Beach Conservation Area. You can explore this site and get a good view of Georgian Bay. The trail will enter Thornbury after another 6 kilometres. You will cross the trestle bridge over Beaver Pond, where you should watch for some...you know...beaver in the pond.

Continue on the trail through Bayview Park. Eventually the trail crosses Highway 26, about 15 kilometres into your ride. Make sure you are very careful when you cross this highway. Follow Lakeshore Drive, staying on the paved road for approximately 2 kilometres, just east of Beaver Street. Rejoin the Georgian Trail and cross over the trestle bridge.

The trail continues on across Grey Road 4 and through Collingwood Township. The trail crosses Blue Mountain Road and soon you will pass through Craigleith at a point about 24 kilometres into your ride. Follow the trail over Osler Bluff Road. The trail will enter Collingwood behind the Blue Mountain Mall. I hope you enjoyed your ride. Turn around and ride it again if you can!

Camping

Fairview Trailer Park (519) 538-2631
Meaford Memorial Park (519) 538-2530

Hotels/Resorts

Bay-Vue Motel (519) 538-3490
Hilltop Motel (519) 538-1700
Trollers (519) 538-3030

For more information contact:

Georgian Triangle Tourist Association
601 First Street
Collingwood, Ontario
L9Y 4L2
(519) 445-7722

1 trail: 3 km

Location:

The Haldimand Conservation Area is located off Lakeshore Road, 6 kilometres east of Nanticoke.

Haldimand Nature Trail

The trail starts just south of the stream and just north of the workshop. You will travel north along the bank of the stream, through areas filled with jewelweed and the ruby-throated hummingbirds that accompany it. The trail crosses the stream at the northern end of the conservation area, loops south and crosses the stream once again. Follow the trail south, take the side trails as an alternate, and you will end up back at the point where you started.

Camping

Haldimand Conservation Area (905) 776-2700
Selkirk Provincial Park (905) 776-2600
Shore Acres Park (2 km west of Port Dover, on Nelson Street)

Hotels/Resorts

Brant Hill Inn (519) 583-1501
Bucks Cottages (519) 583-2263
Erie Beach Hotel (519) 583-1391

For more information contact:

Manager
Long Point Region Conservation Authority
R.R. 3
Simcoe, Ontario
N3Y 4K2
(519) 428-4623

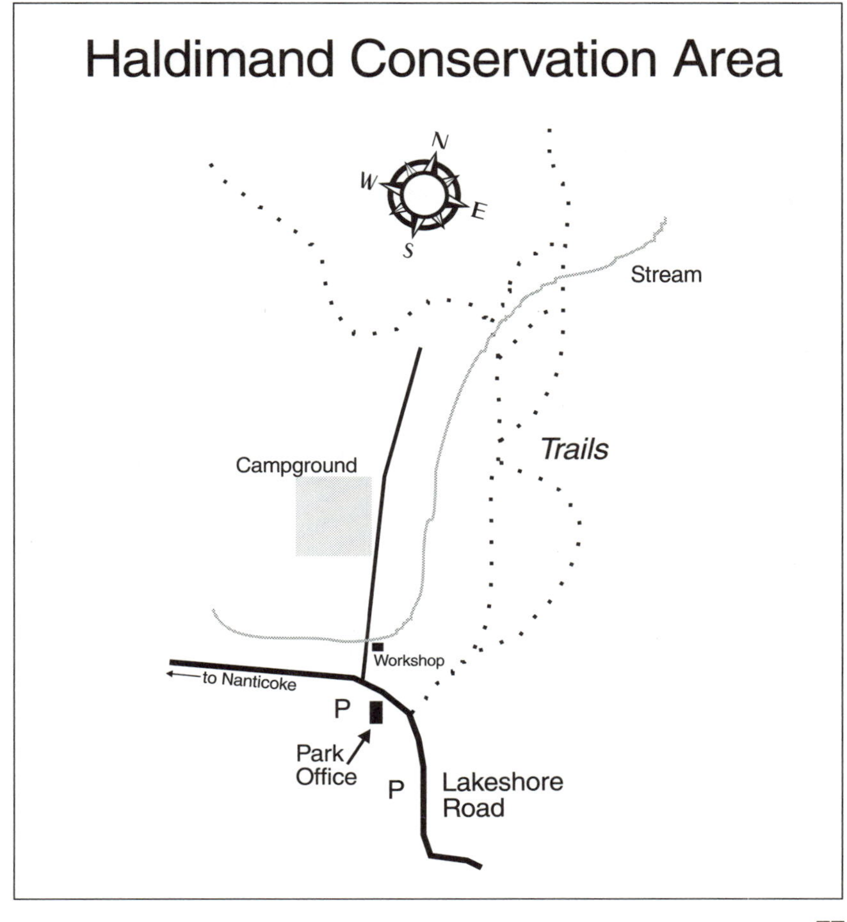
Haldimand Conservation Area
N
W
E
S
Stream
Trails
Campground
Workshop
to Nanticoke
P
Park Office
P
Lakeshore Road

1 trail: 4 km

Location:

Exit Highway 24 onto Radical Road. Follow Radical Road and turn right (south) onto Blueline Road. Enter the conservation area at the ski trail entrance and park your car.

Rating: Easy

Main Trail

This conservation area is located a few miles from the Lake Erie shoreline. Hay Creek was dammed in 1966 and a 5-hectare reservoir was built on the site. Several types of animals inhabit the conservation area, such as raccoons, beavers, skunks, squirrels and rabbits. Some of the bird species found here include woodduck, woodcock, belted kingfisher, great blue heron and ruffed grouse. Ride quietly and you may see some wildlife.

Park your car and follow the access road through the Wildlife Management Area. Once inside the Wildlife Management Area, follow the nature trail northward.

You will be able to see the Hay Creek Reservoir on this trail. The nature trail soon joins up with the access road again. Follow this road northwest and then south until you come to the nature and ski trail.

You can rest at one of the benches and enjoy the scenery if you get tired. Follow the ski trail south and then north until you reach the access road again. Follow the access road back to the ski trail entrance where you parked your car.

Camping

Kamp Kenorus Family Resort (519) 832-5183
MacGregor Point Provincial Park (519) 389-9056
New Fairway Park (519) 389-9800

Hotels/Resorts

Brant Hill Inn (519) 583-1501
Buck's Cottages (519) 583-2263
Erie Beach Hotel (519) 583-1391

For more information contact:

Manager
Long Point Region Conservation Authority
R.R. 3
Simcoe, Ontario
N3Y 4K2
(519) 428-4623

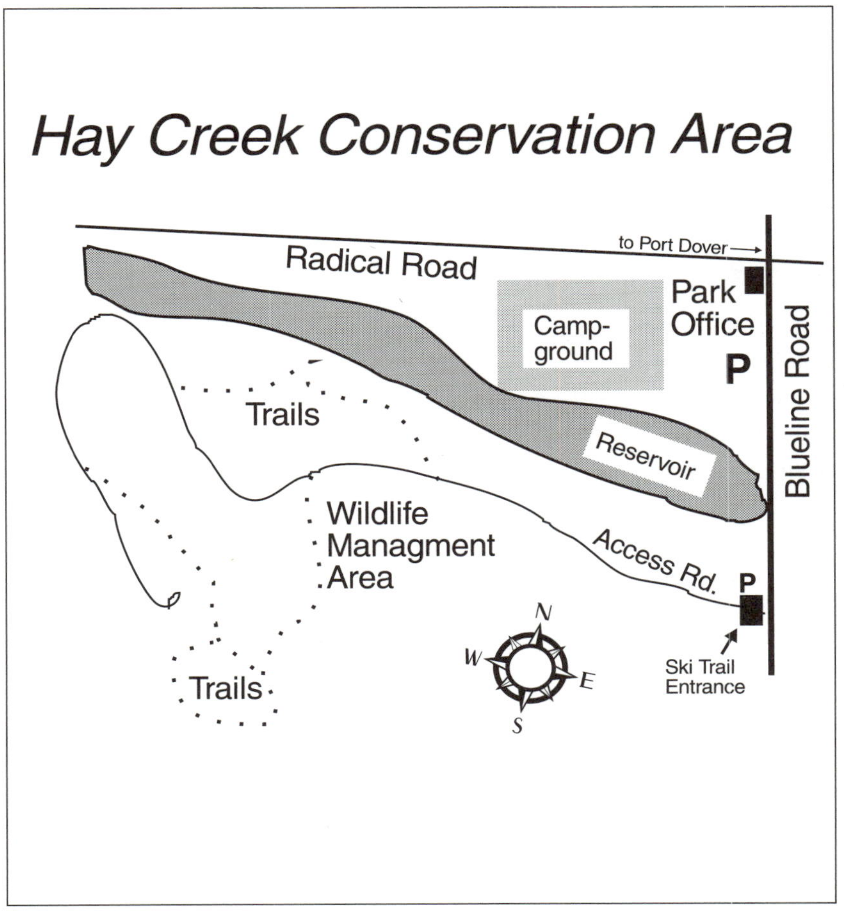

2 trails: 38 km ↔

Location:

Situated just west of the town of Exeter off Highway 83 and Hay Township Concession 4/5.

Rating: Easy/Moderate

Main Trail: 30 km

The trails in Hay Swamp follow logging roads and pass through both deciduous and coniferous forests. They offer an excellent view of this provincially significant wetland. The trail starts at the parking lot at Highway 83 and Hay Township Concession 4/5. Follow the trail north and across the Ausable River. About 2 kilometres into the ride, the trail turns west. Follow the trail westward for approximately 3.5 kilometres. Turn south and follow the trail southeast, then north for several kilometres. The trail then turns east and north again and follows Black Creek. At the edge of the management area, cross Black Creek and ride down the trail on the east side of the creek. After 2 kilometres cross the creek again and backtrack along the trail to the parking lot.

Secondary Trail: 8 km

This trail starts just after the main trail turns west (see map). Follow this trail south and then west. The trail then turns south and ends at Highway 83. Turn around and backtrack to the parking lot. These trails should provide hours of riding enjoyment for any mountain biker, whatever their level of experience.

Camping

Birch Bark Tent and Trailer Park (519) 238-8256
The Pinery Provincial Park (519) 243-2220
Parkhill Conservation Area (519) 294-0114

Hotels/Resorts

Hessenland Country Inn (519) 236-7707
Pinery Inn Resort (519) 243-2474

For more information contact:

Manager
Ausable Bayfield Conservation Authority
P.O. Box 2410,
Exeter, Ontario
N0M 1S7
(519) 235-2610

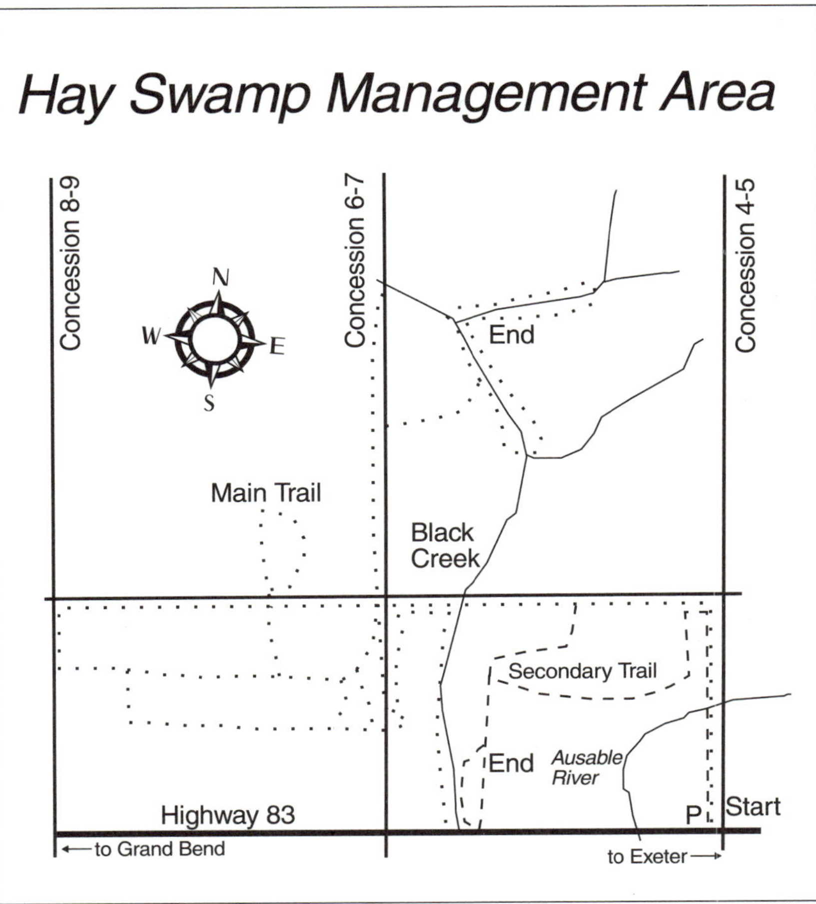

3 trails: 24 km ↔

Location:

This provincial park is located south of Port Elgin. Follow Highway 21 until you reach 4th Concession Road. Follow 4th Concession until you reach Lake Range Road. Follow this road to the park gates and enter the park.

Rating: Moderate/Difficult

Old Shore Road Trail: 12 km

This trail begins at the end of the road to the private cottages. The trail follows the shoreline of Lake Huron to the park boundary. In pioneer days this route provided land transportation between Goderich and Southampton. Today it allows you to avoid park roads to get to the major activity areas of the park. You should pack extra water and some food for this 12-kilometre round-trip ride.

Lake Ridge Trail: 4 km

This trail begins near the end of the main park road (see map). The trail is quite rugged and should only be attempted by excellent mountain bikers. You will experience the ruggedness of the former lake bottom of glacial Lake Nipissing when you climb the former shoreline. Keep your eyes open for evidence of the pioneers who first settled here over one hundred years ago.

The Ducks Unlimited Trail: 8 km

This trail begins at the end of the main park road (see map). Bikes are allowed on this trail as long as they stay off the boardwalk. This trail provides a good view of waterfowl and wildlife. You can see how successful the rehabilitation efforts have been on this former wetland. Watch for the carnivorous pitcher plants in the wetland. Watch out for poison ivy.

Camping

Brucedale Conservation Area (519) 389-4516
MacGregor Point Provincial Park (519) 389-9056
Port Elgin Municipal Tourist Camp (519) 832-2512

Hotels/Resorts

Colonial Motel (519) 832-2021
North Shore Cottages (519) 832-6313
Saugeen Trails Motel (519) 389-4233

For more information contact:

District Manager
Ministry of Natural Resources
611 Ninth Street East
Owen Sound, Ontario
N4K 3E4
(519) 376-3860
or Park Office (519) 389-9056

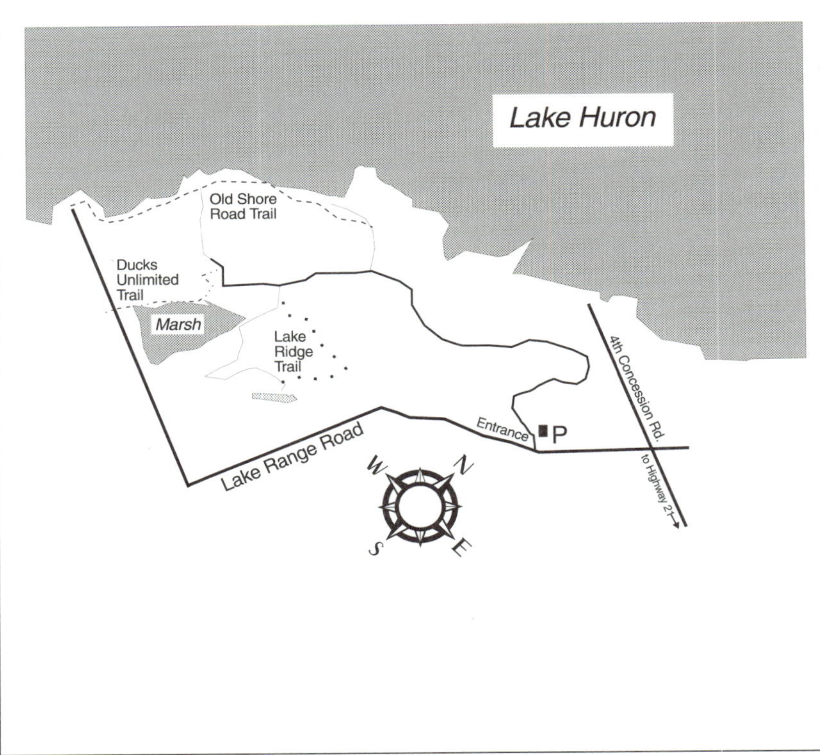

Merritt Trail, St. Catharines

1 trail: 26 km ↔

Location:

This trail runs from Bradley Street in south St. Catharines to Martindale Road in west St. Catharines.

Rating: Moderate

The Trail

Enter the trail at Bradley Street. Follow it until you reach Glendale Avenue. You must take the detour around the railway tracks up Merritt Street and Oakdale Avenue and rejoin the main trail.

The section between Discher Street and Westchester Avenue is one of the most picturesque areas of St. Catharines. You will get an excellent view of the old sections of the Welland Canal on this trail. Continue on the trail until you come to the Centennial Gardens. You may want to take a break and explore these fantastic floral gardens.

The trail continues along Twelve Mile Creek through the site of the old Niagara, St. Catharines & Toronto Railway. Cross Martindale Road and follow the trail until its end at Michigan Avenue. Turn around and go back the way you came.

Camping

Big Valley Campground and Trailer Park (905) 562-5616
Niagara Falls KOA (905) 356-2267
Shangri La Park Campground (905) 562-5851

Hotels/Resorts

Days Inn Prudhommes (905) 562-4101
Howard Johnson's (905) 934-5400
Journey's End Motel (905) 687-8890

For more information contact:

Parks and Recreation Department
320 Geneva Street
P.O. Box 3012
St. Catharines, Ontario
L2R 7C2
(905) 937-7210

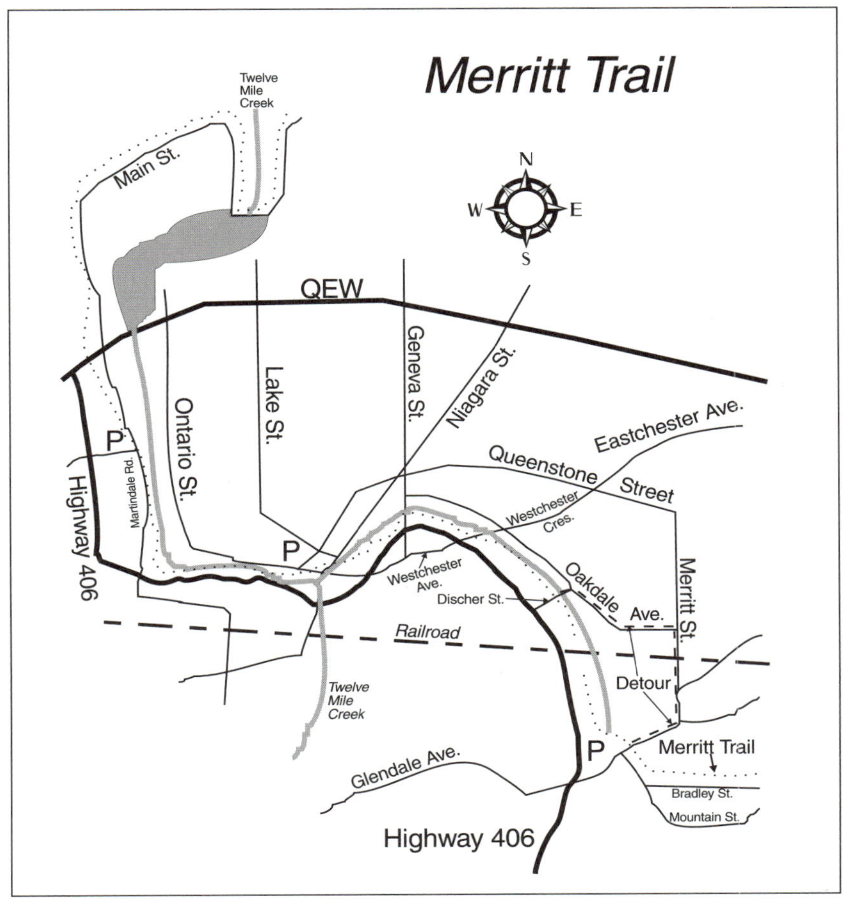

1 trail: 38 km ↔

Location:

This trail starts at the Galt Sewage Treatment Plant in the south end of Cambridge. Exit Highway 401 at the Highway 24 cutoff. Follow Highway 24 south through Cambridge. Turn right and head east at Myers Road in the south end of Cambridge. Leave your car at Churchill Park and ride on the access road to the north end of the park. The trail begins where the abandoned Lake Erie & Northern Railway line cuts through the northern end of Churchill Park.

Rating: Moderate

Paris to Cambridge Trail

The trail starts in Churchill Park. Follow the trail south and out of Cambridge. The trail parallels the Grand River for its entire journey to Paris. The trail follows the route of the now unused Lake Erie & Northern Railway Line. After about 9 kilometres you will enter the town of Glen Morris. This section of the trail between Cambridge and Glen Morris has some rough spots on it. I recommend you ride cautiously on this first section of the trail.

The next 9 kilometres of the trail, between Glen Morris and Paris, are in good shape. Some parts of this section even have stone dust. I think you will enjoy this section of the trail much more than the first section, as it passes through denser brush.

The trail ends in Paris at Washington Street. If you need any bike repairs or supplies, you should visit the Bikeway, located at 300 Grand River Street North in Paris. Their phone number is (519) 442-7545. Thanks goes to Richard Qwerney at the Bikeway for telling me about this trail.

Camping

Barbers Beach (519) 658-9644
Churchill Park (519) 623-1340
Pinehurst Lake Conservation Area (519) 442-4721

Hotels/Resorts

Davidson Motel (519) 442-4417
Journey's End Motel (519) 658-1100
Rose Court Motel (519) 442-2122
Welcome Inns (519) 623-4600

For more information contact:

Grand River Conservation Authority
400 Clyde Road
P.O. Box 729
Cambridge, Ontario
N1R 5W6
(519) 621-2761

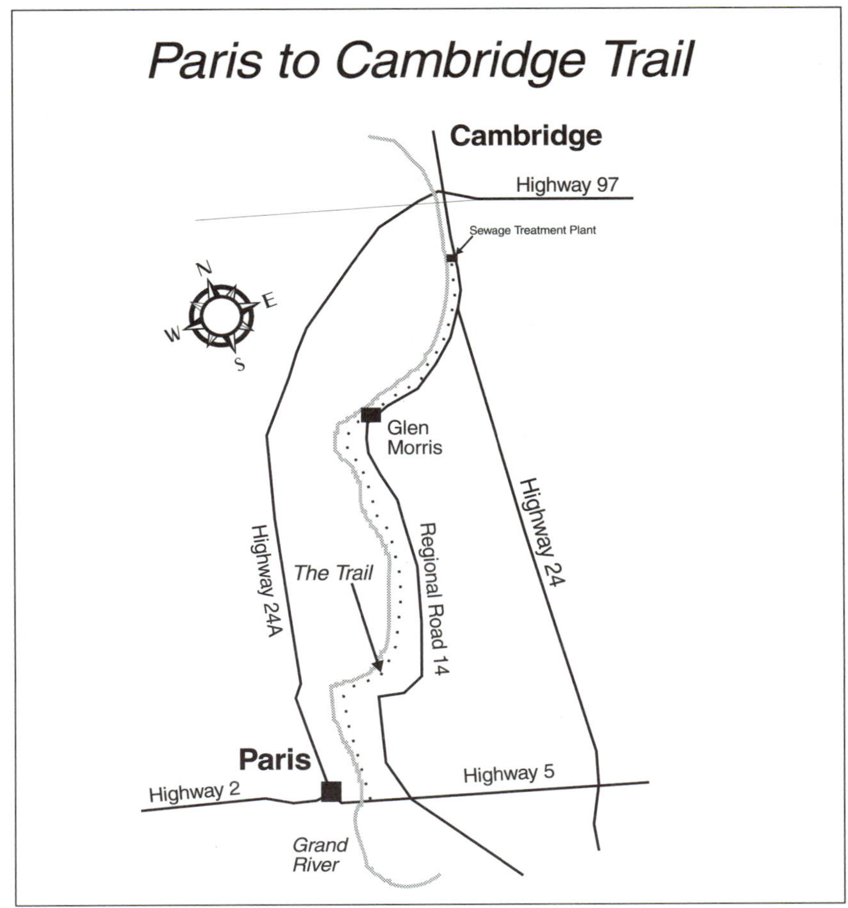

Participark Trail, St. Catharines

1 trail: 4 km ↔

Location:

The east bank of the Twelve Mile Creek from Glendale Avenue to St. Paul Crescent.

Participark Trail

This trail is excellent for mountain bikers who wish to get an excellent workout. The eight exercise stations are spaced intermittently along the trail. You will find complete instructions at each exercise station.

Start the trail at St. Paul Crescent. For a small detour, follow the paved section of the trail under the hydro corridor up to West Park High School. Turn around and backtrack to the main trail. Follow the main trail to its end at Glendale Avenue. Turn around and go back to where you started.

Camping

Big Valley Campground and Trailer Park (905) 562-5616
Niagara Falls KOA (905) 356-2267
Shangri La Park Campground (905) 562-5851

Hotels/Resorts

Days Inn Prudhommes (905) 562-4101
Howard Johnson's (905) 934-5400
Journey's End Motel (905) 687-8890

For more information contact:

Parks and Recreation Department
320 Geneva Street
P.O. Box 3012
St. Catharines, Ontario
L2R 7C2
(905) 937-7210

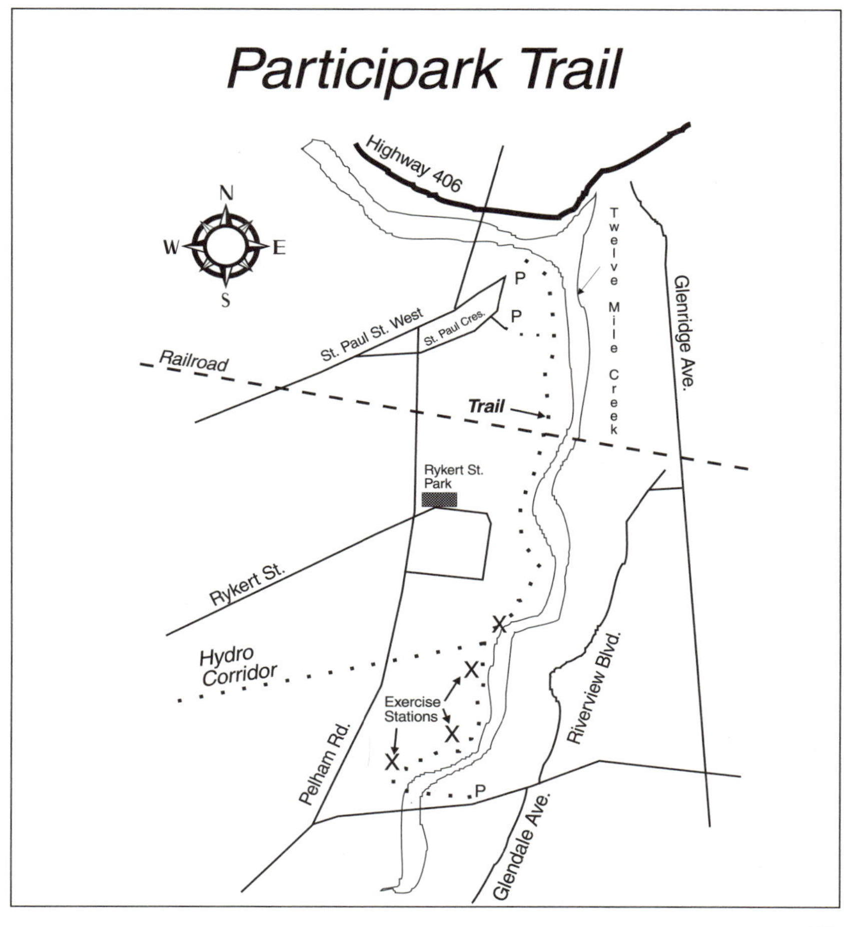
Participark Trail
Highway 406
N
W
E
S
Twelve Mile Creek
Glenridge Ave.
P
P
St. Paul St. West
St. Paul Cres.
Railroad
Trail
Rykert St. Park
Rykert St.
Hydro Corridor
Exercise Stations
Riverview Blvd.
Pelham Rd.
P
Glendale Ave.

2 trails: 23 km ↔

Location:

Exit off Highway 401 at Highway 21 (exit 109). Travel south on Highway 21; it turns into County Road 17. Follow County Road 17 into the park.

Rating: Easy

Marsh Trail: 15 km

The trail starts west of the Rondeau Road picnic area, south of the park store. This 15-kilometre round-trip trail takes you through the middle of an extensive marsh. You can see turtles sunning themselves and great blue heron on the hunt. You may even see an endangered bald eagle! This is a very relaxing mountain-bike ride, so take your time and enjoy the scenery.

Roads in the park: 25 km

The roads in Rondeau Provincial Park are suitable for mountain-bike riding as well.

South Point Trail: 8 km

This trail begins at the south end of Lakeshore Road, or the corner of Rondeau Road and Gardiner Avenue. You can explore the Pointe aux Pins (Point of Pines) or look for the rare prothonotary warbler. This trail lets you enjoy spectacular views of tall pines and the Lake Erie shoreline.

Camping

Rondeau Provincial Park (519) 674-5405

Hotels/Resorts

Johnston's Motel (519) 676-2101
Queen's Motel (519) 676-5477
The Silver Motel (519) 676-5156

Bike Rentals

Bike rentals are available on Harrison Trail just south of Rondeau Avenue. You can rent bikes for an hour, a half day or a full day.

For more information contact:

District Manager
Ministry of Natural Resources
P.O. Box 1168
Chatham, Ontario
N7M 5L8
(519) 354-7340
Park Office (519) 674-5405

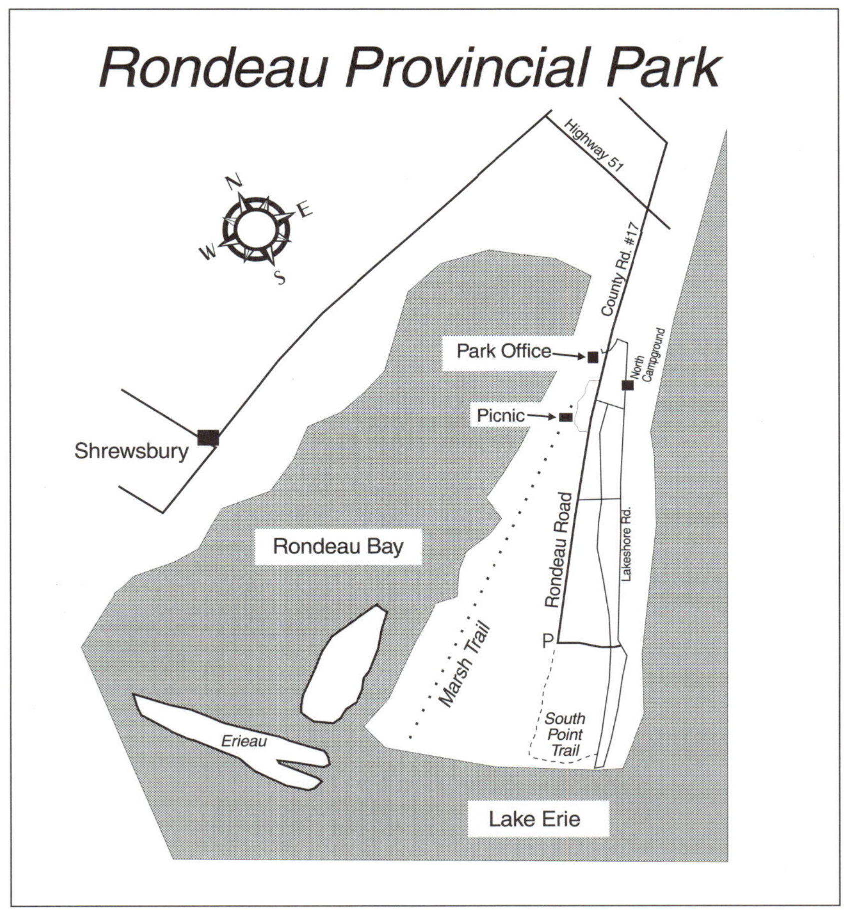

3 trails: 12.5 km

Location:

On the Niagara Escarpment, west of Thorold, in the centre of the Regional Municipality of Niagara. Exit off Highway 406 near Thorold at Beaverdam's Road. Travel west to Merritville Road and turn north, follow it until you reach Decew Road. Travel west on Decew Road until you reach First Street South. Travel north on First Street South until you reach Pelham Road. Head west on Pelham Road until you reach Gilligan Road. Follow Gilligan Road south until you reach the access parking lot for Short Hills Provincial Park on the left-hand side of the road.

Rating: Easy

Central Upland Trail: 2.5 km

This multi-use trail begins on an old logging road allowance at the southern end of Gilligan Road. The trail heads south and rises over a plateau. It turns southwest and crosses over a hydro right of way. The trail then turns northwest, then west, and then north and west again, and finally links up with the Dry Falls Trail. Be careful to stay off any trail branches marked for "walking only" when you ride this trail.

Dry Falls Trail: 5 km

The trail starts at the Pelham Road access point and parallels the west branch of the Twelve Mile Creek to Dry Falls. It returns via an open upland in the centre of the park.

The most prominent feature of the park is the scenic 15-metre waterfall and gorge known as Dry Falls. The falls show the process of differential erosion, by exposing of a large section of the Rochester shale and the Decew dolomite formation of the Niagara Escarpment. Also present are a typical grotto and plunge pool. This is an excellent trail for mountain biking and the view is awesome.

Twelve Mile Creek Trail: 5 km

This trail encircles Camp Wetaskin and follows a large portion of the main branch of the Twelve Mile Creek within the northeast portion of the park. This trail offers many excellent views as well. It is an easy but exciting ride for the novice mountain biker.

Camping

Big Valley Campground and Trailer Park (905) 562-5616
Shangri La Park Campground (905) 562-5851

Hotels/Resorts

Days Inn Prudhommes (905) 562-4101
Journey's End Motel (905) 687-8890

For more information contact:

Ministry of Natural Resources
P.O. Box 1070
Fonthill, Ontario L0S 1E0
(905) 892-2656

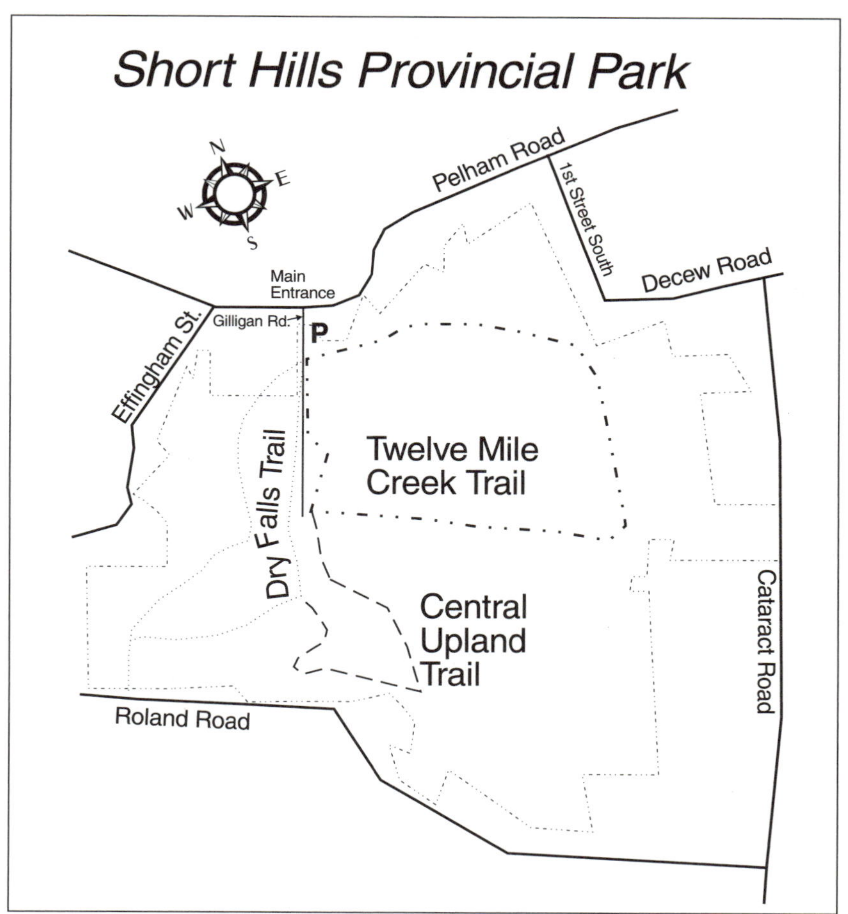

2 trails: 12 km

Location:

This conservation area lies just off Highway 3, about 3 kilometres south of Orwell on County Road 35.

Springwater Forest Trail: 9 km

This trail begins at the parking lot located just off County Road 35. The trail is an excellent place to view a remnant deciduous forest of towering white pines mixed with mature beech trees, white elm, basswood and white oak. If you look carefully along your way you may even see black cherry and sassafras trees. This is also a good location to spot the rare hooded warbler and the pileated woodpecker.

Follow the trail until you come to an observation platform overlooking a marsh. From the top of this platform you can view the small marsh, which was once an open pond. The pond has filled in because of the accumulation of organic matter.

As you cross the stream you should look out for deer and fox; they use it as a watering hole. Several species of plants, such as skunk cabbage and marsh marigold, can only be found near the streams of this conservation area.

The trail eventually brings you near the Springwater Pond, which was used as a trout hatchery in the late 1800s. The trail ends at the parking lot. For an alternate route and to add an extra kilometre to your ride, take the trail along the south end of the pond, which is near the start of the trail (see map).

Jaffa Trail: 3 km

This trail starts at about the halfway point of the Springwater Forest Trail, just after you cross the stream. This trail will take you to the outdoor education centre. There are side trails you should explore on your return trip.

Camping

Dalewood Conservation Area (519) 631-1270
Port Burwell Provincial Park (519) 874-4691
Springwater Conservation Area (519) 773-9037

Hotels/Resorts

Covey Bros. Motel and Family Restaurant (519) 842-7366
Journey's End Motel, St. Thomas (519) 633-4082

For more information contact:

Manager
Catfish Creek Conservation Authority
R.R. 5
Aylmer, Ontario
N5H 2R4
(519) 773-9037

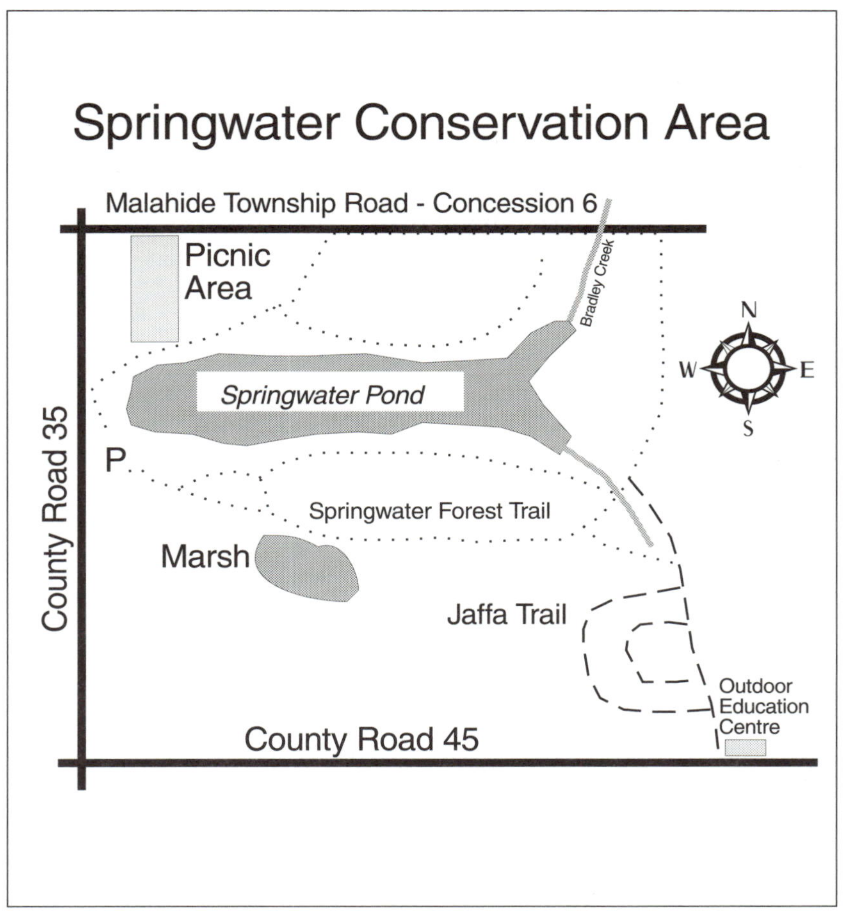

1 trail: 3 km ↔

Location:

Central St. Catharines. Enter off Carlton Street or Geneva Street.

Terry Fox Trail: 3 km

This trail has six exercise stations for those of you who want a better workout. You will find complete instructions at each exercise station. You can start this trail at either end, because of the unique design of this fitness trail. You can park at any of the parking lots located on the trail map.

Camping

Big Valley Campground and Trailer Park (905) 562-5616
Niagara Falls KOA (905) 356-2267
Shangri La Park Campground (905) 562-5851

Hotels/Resorts

Days Inn Prudhommes (905) 562-4101
Howard Johnson's (905) 934-5400
Journey's End Motel (905) 687-8890

For more information contact:

Parks and Recreation Department
320 Geneva Street
P.O. Box 3012
St. Catharines, Ontario
L2R 7C2
(905) 937-7210

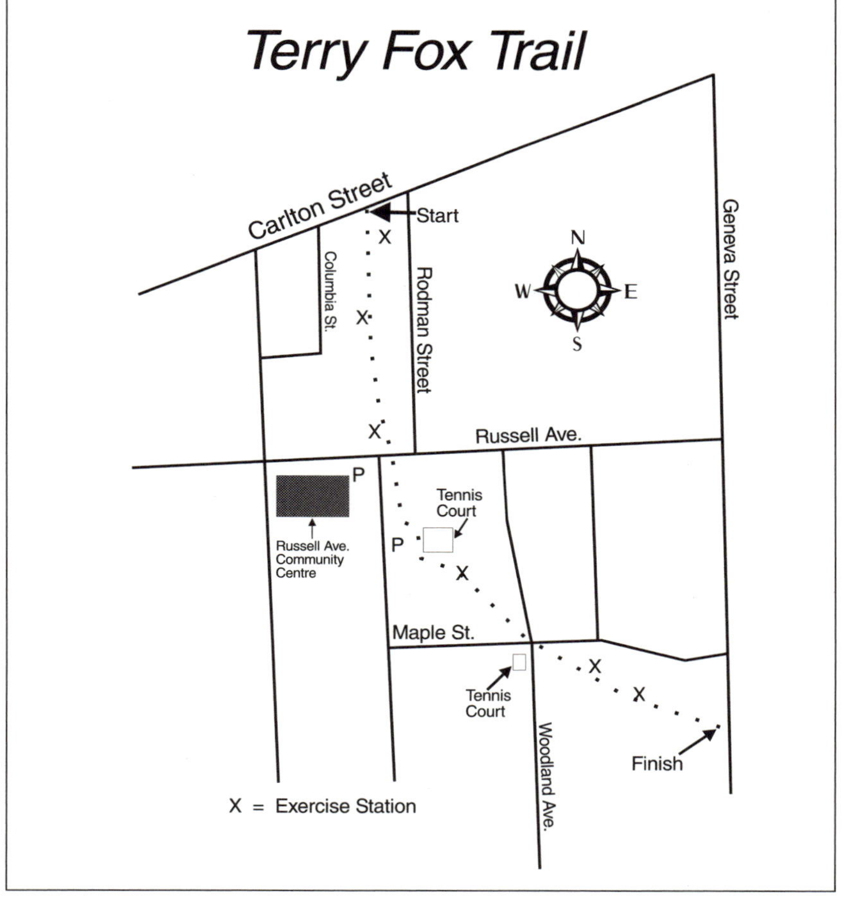
Terry Fox Trail
Carlton Street
Start
Columbia St.
Rodman Street
Geneva Street
N
W
E
S
Russell Ave.
P
Tennis Court
Russell Ave. Community Centre
P
Maple St.
Tennis Court
Woodland Ave.
Finish
X = Exercise Station

1 trail: 5 km ↔

Location:

Along Walker's Creek from Linwell Road to Cindy Drive.

Rating: Easy

Walker's Creek Trail

Parking is available at the Grantham YMCA located just off Linwell Road. The trail starts behind the YMCA building. Follow the trail along the banks of Walker's Creek. You may want to use the two exercise stations along the trail. The trail ends at Cindy Drive. If you enjoyed it, backtrack and ride it again.

Camping

Big Valley Campground and Trailer Park (905) 562-5616
Niagara Falls KOA (905) 356-2267
Shangri La Park Campground (905) 562-5851

Hotels/Resorts

Days Inn Prudhommes (905) 562-4101
Howard Johnson's (905) 934-5400
Journey's End Motel (905) 687-8890

For more information contact:

Parks and Recreation Department
320 Geneva Street
P.O. Box 3012
St. Catharines, Ontario
L2R 7C2
(905) 937-7210

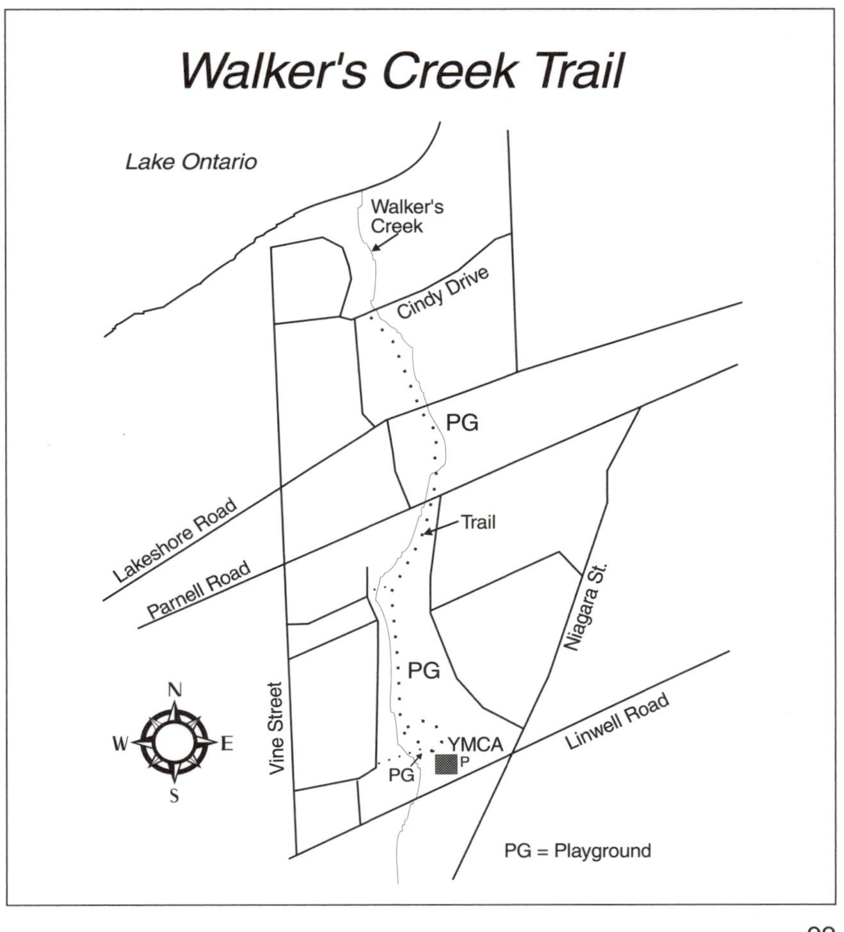
Walker's Creek Trail
Lake Ontario
Walker's Creek
Cindy Drive
PG
Trail
Lakeshore Road
Parnell Road
Niagara St.
PG
Vine Street
YMCA
P
PG
Linwell Road
N
W
E
S
PG = Playground

4 km of trails

Location:

The Wawanosh Valley Conservation Area is located off County Road 22, west of Blyth.

Rating: Easy

The Trails

Park in the lot provided and start the trail on the west side of Belgrave Creek. Follow the trail through the coniferous plantation and into the cedar lowland and then over the creek. Follow the trail northeast through the marsh area and into the cedar and hemlock woodlot. The trail then heads southeast into a mixed deciduous woodlot.

Continue on the trail as it travels through a field with tree and hedge-row plantings until you return to the cedar lowlands. Cross the creek and ride back to your car. You could vary the ride by taking some of the branch trails. I hope you enjoy this short but exciting ride.

Camping

Falls Reserve Conservation Area (519) 524-6429
Lake Huron Resort (519) 524-6438
Shelter Valley Trailer Park (519) 524-4141

Hotels/Resorts

Benmiller Inn (519) 524-2191
Cedar Lodge Motel (519) 524-8379
Maple Leaf Motel (519) 524-2302

For more information contact:

Communications Co-ordinator
Maitland Valley Conservation Area
P.O. Box 127
Wroxeter, Ontario
N0G 2X0
(519) 335-3557

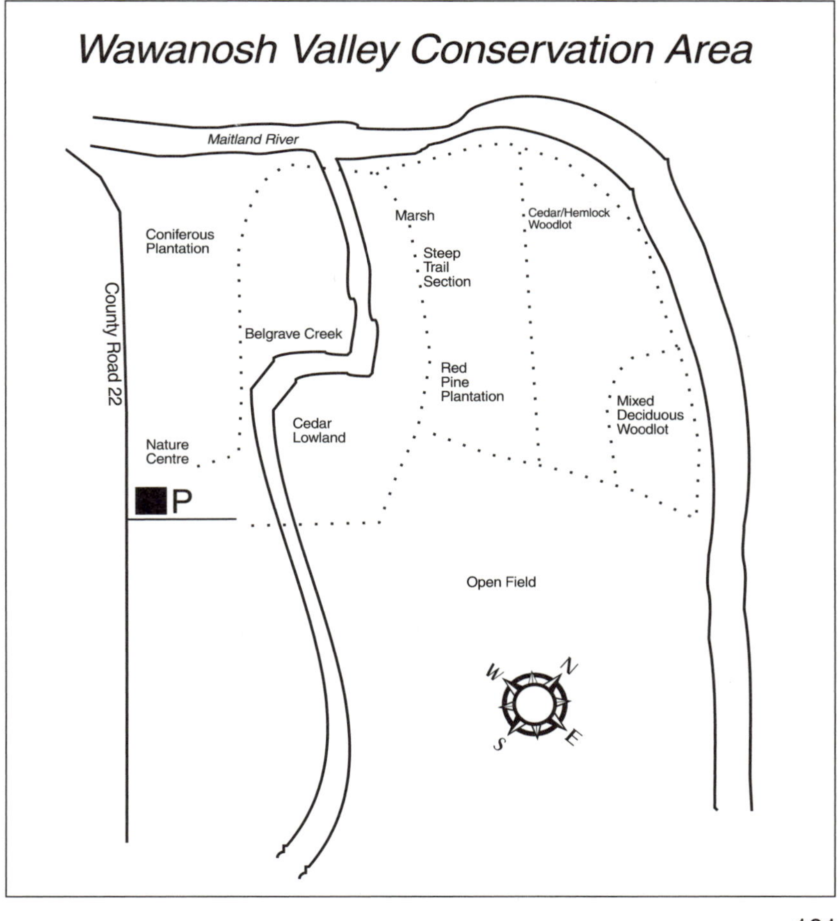
Wawanosh Valley Conservation Area
Maitland River
Coniferous Plantation
County Road 22
Belgrave Creek
Nature Centre
P
Cedar Lowland
Marsh
Steep Trail Section
Red Pine Plantation
Cedar/Hemlock Woodlot
Mixed Deciduous Woodlot
Open Field
W
N
S
E